The Messages

The Messages

A Memoir

by

Dawn Kohler

Published in the United States of America
by Train of Thought Press

ISBN: 978-0-9992488-4-3

eBook: ISBN: 978-0-9992488-5-0

Library of Congress Control Number: 2021949516

Excerpts from this book where previously published in the
author's memoir, *A New Dawn Rising, One Woman's Spiritual
Odyssey*

INTRODUCTION

I came into the world two weeks late and my father named me Dawn. My mother wanted to call me Marie, after his mother whom she didn't like, but my father insisted on the name. He said he had a dream one night that he was going to have a daughter, and the name came with the vision. It was an unusual statement for my father to make. He was after all a gruff, pragmatic, atheist. But I suppose him naming me was one of the reasons I was my father's daughter. At least that's what I believed growing up.

I had other beliefs as a child too. I believed my mother, a young, coalminers-daughter from West Virginia was ill equipped to raise me in San Diego in the 1960s. And that despite her, I was determined to survive my childhood. I had a fierce knowing that I had something to do in this life, and I told her so often.

Based on my father's gene pool I was raised with a strong German work ethic, so for a while what I thought I had to do in life was work. My first official job was at Sea World working the popcorn stand outside of the dolphin show. A year later, I bagged groceries for a supermarket chain and ran deliveries, mostly reports and blood samples for a medical laboratory. I was also regularly ditching school with my friends to hang out at the beach. And I got into my fair share of trouble for not adhering to trespassing signs and speed limits.

In my senior year of high school, I watched a few friends lose their lives to drugs, alcohol, and car accidents. At that point, I decided to apply my thrill seeking towards my career instead of my demise. I got my Real Estate License and sold houses to help me get through business school. When I graduated, I moved to San Francisco with my high school boyfriend and sold computers for an Apple dealer. The following year he asked me to marry him. I said yes, not because I was madly in love, but because we had been together for over 8 years and by then you either got married or broke up. I was not willing to do the latter. He had become a part of me, I didn't want to lose.

During that same year we also quit our jobs and started a small computer service company. The industry was booming, and the company grew fast. Our lives together were blossoming and for the next seven years we expanded our staff to over 60 employees, and I gave birth to 3 beautiful children.

Then the shift happened. In my early thirties, my childhood knowing emerged as an irrevocable calling that required a great deal of work. But not the kind of work I had known or could have ever imagined.

I am, at my core, a reasonable, rational person so this true story is difficult to share. What you are about to read divulges personal experiences I wish I did not have to divulge. It also reveals spiritual experiences that I resisted, even as they intelligently guided me on a healing journey that led to encounters where I was summoned to write. In those encounters, I was taking dictation, there was no two-way dialogue and what was communicated to me is nothing I would have personally written. If that sounds strange to you, don't worry. It sounds strange to me too. I have no religious upbringing or orientation for this, nor was this a conversion to any religion. It was not drug or alcohol induced in any way. It was also not a love and light kind of experience either. There was healing, but it was not easily obtained.

To this day it is difficult for me to grasp the magnitude of these messages. But I owe it to the life that supports me, and to the light that continuously appeared to me on this journey directing me to "write the book".

I originally wrote the story and self-published it in 1999 under the title *A New Dawn Rising*. In this new version, I added a modern-day narrative as I share the story with my grown daughter. I am 60 years old now, and these remain the most profound experiences of my life.

To maintain anonymity, I have changed the names of individuals and places, and in some cases consolidated minor characters and therapy sessions to help create a more efficient recount of the story. Besides those changes, I have communicated the journey as clearly as I experienced it.

CHAPTER ONE

June 2021

The afternoon the manuscript arrived I was in the yard with Katie. The wedding was only a week away and we had spent the day planting fresh flowers at the edge of the lawn and trimming the hedges behind the patio.

The carrier pounded on the front door several times.

"Come around back," I yelled from the yard.

A moment later his head appeared above the fence as Katie walked up to the gate.

"Are you Dawn Kohler?"

"No, I'm her daughter."

"That's good enough for me. Sign here please."

I took off my gardening gloves and walked up to the gate. "What's this?"

"Probably something for the wedding," Katie said. "Can we take a break? I need some water."

"Sure," I said as I shook the padded envelope.

We walked back to the yard. I slipped off my shoes and went upstairs to the kitchen. Katie tossed down her gardening gloves and followed me.

"Who's the package from?" She pulled a pitcher out of the refrigerator and poured us iced tea. Her long red hair flowing down her slender back, moving as carefree and grace-ful as she did.

"I don't know. I don't recognize the address."

"Open it," she said as she sat down next to me at the rustic wood kitchen table.

I wove my fingernail under the seal and stripped open the envelope. Inside was an old manuscript I wrote, and a note from somebody I once knew.

"What is it?" Katie asked.

I stared at the pages as those years flooded back to me like an unfinished calling. I remembered receiving the mes-sages like it happened yesterday, and the terrifying vision I was shown of our humanity that has haunted me ever since. We still have time to avoid the suffering though. That was made clear to me. My throat tightened.

"Did you write this?" Katie asked.

"Yes, I did."

"What's it about? And who is the note from?"

I looked out the window toward the ocean. Katie was just a baby when it all began, and I had never told the kids what really happened back then.

"It's a long story," I said.

"If it means we can stop doing yard work, I'd love to hear it." She stood up from the kitchen table and walked toward the refrigerator.

"Can I open a bottle of wine?" she asked.

"Probably a good idea."

I looked at the manuscript and wondered how much of what had happened I should share with Katie. She was the youngest of my three children, but she was an old soul for a 26-year-old and the most likely to understand the extraordi-nary journey.

She poured me a glass of wine and then filled hers. My heart told me it was time to tell her about what happened to me, and *The Messages* I received during those three nights in May.

CHAPTER TWO

September 1992

The Santa Ana winds that usually marked September had died away, and a heavy fog hugged the Southern California coastline that morning. I jumped out of bed and made my way to the walk-in closet. A journalist from the *Los Angeles Times* was coming to do a cover story on our company. The editor was intrigued by our rapid success in the computer industry and our status as a woman-owned business. I was feeling numb about the interview. A month earlier, I had awoken into a peculiar sensation. It felt like a small white comet had emerged in my chest and was hovering over my heart, summoning me like a draft card. I considered myself to be a secular businesswoman, but by some primordial instinct every cell in my body was telling me that I was receiving a calling.

I pulled my black shoes off the rack and reached for my olive-green suit.

"Dawn, have you seen my keys?" Jeff yelled from downstairs.

"Be right down." I rushed to put on my slacks and a silk blouse. When I turned to leave the bedroom, Jeff was standing in the doorway, his sandy brown hair and broad shoulders filling its frame.

"I always hang them on the key rack when I come home from the beach," he said as he pushed out his barreled chest, accusing me with his boyish blue eyes.

I searched my memory as if I were ransacking a kitchen. Did I take his car last night? Did I open the door to remove the kids' car seats?

"I'll find them," I said as I ran downstairs. I looked across the white-tile counter next to the stove. In the center were his keys; on the same gold key ring I gave him in high school. I held them up as he grabbed them from behind me.

"Thank you," he said as he took them from my hand. "What time are you coming into the office?"

"I'll be there as soon as I drop off Jen at kindergarten."

"Better hurry. The interview with the *Los Angeles Times* is at nine, and the barbeque starts at noon."

The office barbeque always started at noon on Fridays. That was my cue to leave so the work atmosphere would shift from getting things done to Jeff leading the computer technicians in his weekly beer-drinking, poker-playing, dart-throwing, steak and sausage feast in the warehouse. Jeff was the life of the party, which is one of the things I loved about him. He brought levity to my striving, while my determination brought structure to his otherwise playful world.

"Please don't start the barbeque until after the reporter leaves."

"Are you kidding? I'm going to invite him for a beer and show him the real work we do."

"Jeff..."

"Just kidding, dear," he said as he pulled me in by my waist and gave me a kiss goodbye.

"Mom, come on, let's get ready," Jen grabbed my hand to pull me upstairs. Her blonde hair was falling from a loose braid. Her eyes were as blue as Jeff's, her pug nose wrinkling as she smiled.

"What's your hurry?" I asked.

"My teacher is bringing in her new baby today."

"Wow. Then we better get moving," I said as I looked across the room to Isabella, an El Salvadorean refugee who we sponsored as a nanny. Isabella was just a few years older than Jeff and me and she covered the kids with us like a third parent, showing up every Monday in a bright colored tee shirt and a shameless smile that revealed a silver capped tooth.

Isabella picked up two-year-old Matthew from in front of the television while Katie laid asleep in her crib.

"You go, Dawn, you go. Mi play con las bebés," she said as she tickled Matthew until he belly laughed.

I dropped Jen off at school and by the time I arrived at work the media truck was already there. A light was set up in front of the steel and glass building and the photographer was setting up his cameras. Trying to ignore the spiraling energy hovering in my chest, I pulled into my parking space and quickly went into the building. Angie, our lanky, just-out-of-college office manager greeted me as I walked through the door.

"Your morning reports are on your desk and the guy doing the interview is waiting for you in the conference room."

"Thank you. Please tell him I will be right there."

I walked past the staff into my office, pulled my phone messages out of the inbox and swiveled in my high-back leather chair toward my desk.

"Dawn, they're ready for you," Angie's voice came over the intercom. I quickly glanced over the reports on my desk and then walked into the conference room.

The reporter stood when I entered. He was an older gentleman in a dark blue suit with graying hair and thick glasses that rested in the middle of his large rosy nose. We exchanged pleasantries and sat down. His questions were quick and predictable: why did we start the company; what made us different; what was it like to be a female CEO? My answers were succinct as I sat poised in my chair, feeling as if I were talking to him through an ill-fitted costume, in a role I was no longer to play.

As we wrapped up the interview, he put down his pen and leaned back in his chair. "So, what's next?" he asked. "Where do you plan to take the company from here?"

The energy in my chest flared as he spoke, "I'm not sure," I said as I cleared my throat. "Right now, we are focused on giving our customers the best support in the market."

My words tasted like dry paste. Sentences that no longer had meaning. And the future, something I had always been able to envision, now looked like a free fall into a bottomless canyon.

My anxiety escalated that weekend. Hoping to exhaust my fears, and the relentless spiritual summons that hovered underneath them, I stayed as active as possible. I put Katie in a stroller and ran her to the beach. I took Matthew to a birthday party, went grocery shopping at two markets, and then went to the mall to buy a gift for my mother. Still feeling the high-voltage energy, I went to the community pool and swam for an hour.

By Sunday, Jeff was looking at me like I was on something illegal. "Why don't you sit down," he asked as he sat in the playroom watching a baseball game with the kids.

"I can't relax. I have to keep moving."

"I'll keep you moving," he said with a grin. I ignored the innuendo and went downstairs to make dinner.

Jen walked into the kitchen as I was preparing the meal. She crawled up on the barstool and quietly watched me as I chopped vegetables for the soup. Her blonde bangs falling to the side of her brow. Her eyes filled with a sensitive intelligence not yet constructed into words. She stared at me for several moments.

"What's up baby? Are you okay?" I asked.

"Yeah. It just feels weird tonight."

"What feels weird?" I asked.

"The air feels weird." She started to giggle, "Mom, can air feel weird?"

"Yes, baby. Air can feel weird. Are you worried about something?"

"No, it's not inside of me. It's inside the air."

I nodded. "Maybe tomorrow the air will feel better."

"Maybe," she said as she looked at me with concern.

In the morning I jumped out of bed, fed the kids, then drove into work, every mile seeming like I was going further and further in the wrong direction. I pulled up to the building and reached for the car door when a warm flush waved over me, and suddenly I couldn't move. My fingers would not open the handle. I took a deep breath. I had the strength, desire, and the ability, but something inside of me wasn't allowing me to move. I tried again to pull the door lever and my fingers didn't budge. The spirit in my body was holding me hostage not allowing me to get out of the car.

For the next twenty minutes, I tried to will myself to open the car door, to walk into the building, to get on with my life as I knew it. Yet, with every attempt, an inaudible message repeated in my mind.

This is no longer your way.

This is no longer your way.

I pounded my fist on the steering wheel then hit the side of the door.

"I want it to be my way!" I yelled at the sky. I hit the door a few more times then collapsed over the wheel. My fight to maintain my life as I knew it, turned into a feeling of utter defeat. I slowly moved toward my keys, turned on the car and drove home.

When I got back to the house, I slid off my shoes and dragged myself up the stairs. Isabella stood at the top with Katie in her arms.

"Estás enfermo?" she asked.

"No sé, Isabella, no sé."

Katie reached for me and I carried her into my room. We played on the floor for a bit then Isabella came in and picked her up.

"Mi go to the park con Matthew y Katie."

"Si, Isabella. Thank you."

When Isabella and the kids left, I crawled into bed as if I weighed a thousand pounds. My eyes slammed shut and suddenly I saw myself falling into an abyss. A sense of emptiness filled my body leaving a void so large I could barely speak. I laid there for the next several days claiming to have the flu. By Sunday, Jeff was starting to worry.

"Isabella thinks you are pregnant again," he said that morning as he sat on the edge of the bed.

"No, I'm not pregnant."

"Then let's take the kids to the beach. The fresh air will make you feel better."

"Can you please take them," I said. "I just want to lay here."

"This is starting to get weird. What's happening to you?"

"I don't know. But it feels big."

"You're not dying, are you?"

"No. I'm not dying. But I think God wants me to do something."

"I think God wants you to go to the beach with me and the kids."

"It feels like more than that," I said as I shook my head and fell back into bed.

"Ok, but I don't think you are going to find out lying here under the covers."

"Trust me, if I could get up I would."

The following week, I only got out of bed to do what was necessary for the children. Other than that, I would toss and turn, feeling the energy spiraling in my chest, becoming clearer and clearer that I was receiving a calling without any sense of what I was being summoned to do, or how it was about to change my life. As I sank deeper into despair, I started to pray for a direction.

A few nights later, I felt Jeff standing over me. I tugged my eyes open and looked up at him. His light blue eyes verged on tears.

He pulled his hand out of his pocket and handed me a business card.

"I found this in your car," he said. "I think you should call her."

I looked at the card, *Anne Myers, Psychotherapist.*

I had gone to a medical doctor shortly after the energy in my chest began to flare and the rising anxiety it seemed to trigger. After a battery of tests, the doctor said there was nothing physically wrong with me and handed me Anne's card. Having no desire to go to therapy, I wadded up the card and threw it in the back seat hoping it would go out with the trash.

"We can't keep living like this," he said.

I gave him an empty stare. "Okay," I said. "I'll call her."

The following week, I sat in the small lobby of Anne Myers' office staring at a tea table pushed up against the grass-cloth wall. Piano solos playing from a ceiling speaker glazed over the heavy silence. Down the narrow hall were four dark oak doors, all of them closed. I dropped my head back on the worn, stuffed chair. How did my life lead me here, to a psycho-therapist's office that felt like a dead end to a promising road?

A moment of silence, a fleeting thought to leave, then my mother's voice in her Southern accent came crashing through my thoughts, advice I'd heard for everything from a bad dream to my acute appendicitis, 'You're fine. It's all in your head. You just need something to do to keep you busy.' My father's stern, deep voice chimed in after hers, so ingrained in my mind I thought it to be my own, 'Dawn, there are people in the world with real problems, and you're not one of them.'

I heard a door open and footsteps came down the hall. I sat up straight, my darkening blonde hair falling onto the broad-padded shoulders of my silk navy-blue business suit, my athletic body worn down to fair skin on stubborn bones.

A sable haired woman in her late thirties appeared. "Hi, are you Dawn?"

"Yes."

"My name is Anne. Why don't you come back to my office?"

I stared at her before I stood up. She was a short, medium-built woman wearing a pink and white striped cotton dress that somehow didn't suit her angular face, dark olive-tone skin and long, wavy hair. She teetered nervously on her toes. It was an awkward moment. I pulled myself up to greet her, stood tall, straightened my shoulders, and walked down the hall before her.

We walked back into a small but comfortable office. A narrow walnut desk was angled against one wall; a rose-colored couch paralleled the other. A large leather chair stood in front of a bay window that looked upon an aspen tree in full bloom. The room was decorated in soft floral and the walls painted a warm shade of pink. I tossed my keys on the end table and sat down on the couch.

"Would you like a cup of tea or coffee?"

"No, thank you."

She picked up a tea bag and bounced it in a cup of hot water.

"You said on the phone that you were referred by Dr. Barns."

Our eyes met and Anne's shoulders let down. She took a deep breath and released it softly. She asked me a few questions about my work, family, and general health then asked about my symptoms. I briefly mentioned the unexplainable energy hovering in my chest, while focusing on the more tangible feelings of anxiety and depression.

"So, there you have it," I said. "What's your diagnosis?"

Anne took a sip of her tea and looked across the distance between us warmly, almost enchanted. "I don't give diagnoses. I don't know what's wrong with you any more than you do."

I looked at my keys and thought about leaving.

"Dawn, your mind is trying to tell you something, and it's using your body to get your attention. It will take some time and dedication on both our parts to determine what's causing your symptoms."

"How much time?"

"With weekly sessions it could take months, maybe years."

"Years? You've got to be kidding."

"Therapy takes time."

"What's the short cut?"

She smiled and her eyes continued to soften. "Unfortunately, there is no short cut. If you really want relief, it's going to take some time."

Her tone was disarming, and I didn't want to be disarmed.

"Am I allowed to ask you questions?"

"Sure. What would you like to know?"

"How long have you been a therapist?"

"About three years."

"Are you married?"

"Yes, I've been married for...let's see...about ten years."

"Any kids?"

"No, we decided not to."

"Was that difficult?"

"Yes, I think about it at times, but there are so many adult children in the world who need help I decided that being a therapist was where my energy could provide the best service." She took another sip of her tea then shifted the focus back on me.

"What is it you would like to achieve in therapy?" she asked. "Is there a goal you would like to accomplish?"

"I want to know what this energy in my chest is about. What does it want from me?"

"Tell me more."

I took a deep breath. "I know it sounds strange, but I think I am receiving some kind of calling."

"That doesn't sound strange. How do you experience it?"

"I woke up one morning to this energy in my body that hovers in my chest like a spiraling comet. And it doesn't feel like it's coming from me."

Anne looked as if she were absorbing my words. I felt listened to and continued. "And it's insistent. It's like by some primordial instinct, I know I am being called to do something. Something that is greater than me."

She put down her tea and leaned forward. The distance between us had narrowed and the air around us felt good, warm.

"Do you have any religious affiliations?"

"No, and I don't want any. I am a practical businesswoman. Honestly, I don't know what God would want with me."

She smiled. "How about your parents?"

I told her that my father was raised Catholic and hates Catholicism and my mother took us to a Presbyterian church one day to be baptized 'just in case' and we never went again.

She looked up at me after writing something down. "Can you tell me a little more about your parents? What your relationship was like with them as a child?"

I shook my head. "Anne, I'm here because this energy in my chest is telling me I have to do something now. And it feels incredibly significant. I don't really want to waste time talking about my parents or my past."

She looked at me gently and put down her pen. "I believe you are receiving some sort of a calling. What you describe seems very real. And I also believe we need to understand who we are, and how our lives have affected us in order to discover and fulfill our life purpose."

"But this is greater than me."

"I'm sure it is. However, we have to start with you."

I felt unarmed by her, as if every time I drew my sword, she would tenderly remove it with words I could understand, with compassion I had not known. I nodded.

"Tell me about your parents."

I took a deep breath and leaned back on the couch. "They were normal," I said. "My mom wasn't really a factor in my life. We're closer now that I've had children, but when I was young there was no real connection. I have always felt like I raised myself."

"What about your father?"

I laughed, though I didn't know why. If I really felt like opening up to her, I would have told her that my dad was the one who raised me. We had a connection I never had with my mother. He was the one who went to my high school tennis matches, and he was always eager to talk to me about my various part-time jobs through school. We'd laugh at jokes nobody else in the family would get, and discuss world events nobody else in the family was interested in.

I looked up at Anne. It seemed like everything that I had worked for in my life, I had worked for to make my dad proud. But things had changed. He hadn't spoken to me much since I married Jeff. He liked Jeff, but I had a strange sense that my marriage somehow betrayed him.

"My dad helped me out," I said. "When he approved of what I was doing he would help out financially and give me encouragement. And when he didn't approve, he'd just stop talking to me."

"That must have hurt."

"No, not really. I wasn't affected by my parents."

She paused, looking at me like she wanted me to say more, but I had nothing more to say.

"Did either one of them use drugs or alcohol?"

I hesitated. "Does wine count?"

"Last time I checked."

"My mother's a wine drinker."

"Was it excessive?"

"At times," I said.

"Did that bother you?"

"I don't know. I guess I told her to stop a few times."

"And did she?"

I smirked. "Yes. She stopped drinking out of wine glasses and started drinking out of coffee mugs."

"How did that make you feel?"

"Like the wine was more important than I was."

"That's a very sad statement. Why did you say it with a smile?"

"It wasn't that big a deal. Anyway, like I said, I raised myself."

She tilted her head as if she didn't quite believe me, and then wrote something down on her note pad. "That's interesting, that as a little girl you made the decision to raise yourself. Why do you think you made it?"

"I don't know and what does it matter? Anne, I'm receiving a calling that has something to do with the future. That's what's behind this energy. I can feel it in every cell in my body. And like I said, I really don't want to waste time on the past. That seems totally irrelevant."

"I think it is very relevant. A true spiritual calling returns us to our nature. We have to go home to who we are in order to return to the world with any kind of truly authentic gift. The anxiety and depression you are experiencing is from an unresolved past, and the unresolved past is always in the present. Whatever you are being called to do lies beneath it."

I stared at her, and she gently asked the question again.

"Why do you think you made the decision to raise yourself?"

"My mother didn't seem very competent, and I felt that I was somehow smarter than she was, so I just started to take care of myself."

"How old were you?"

"Around 5 years old. Since then, it's always felt safer to stay on my own."

"What about your husband and children?"

"I take care of my children--they don't take care of me. And Jeff and I are very self-sufficient. We make good partners, but we do just as well on our own."

"What about your needs?"

"I don't have needs."

She put down her pen and looked at me. Her eyes were large, a muted blue with a gaze more loving than perceptive.

"Can you remember the last time you got upset or cried?"

"No, and there are two things about me that you should probably know. I don't cry, and I don't throw up."

"You've, never thrown up?"

"Once, but that was because my appendix burst."

"It sounds like you have a great deal of self-control."

"It's better than losing it."

She looked at me, then again wrote notes on her clipboard.

"Dawn, at one point in your existence you were a feeling child, fully alive and in tune with your needs and emotions. Somewhere along the line, you were emotionally injured. If you were not safe to feel your pain, you began to control it, and by doing so you cut yourself off from the natural flow of your emotions. We all have needs, and denying their existence doesn't make them go away, it only stuffs them down to be dealt with later."

She was listening to me in a way that I had never experienced. Seeking to understand me instead of dismissing my fears and concerns as trivial.

"I don't know if this is related," I said, "but when I was young, in elementary school, I remember I used to go into the bathroom and look at myself in the mirror. I would stare into my eyes and ask myself who I am. But I didn't know. I couldn't see anybody in my body. It freaked me out so much I would panic and run away from my own reflection."

"Why do you think you did that?"

"I don't know. I was probably just a weird kid."

"Did you ever tell your mother about it?"

"No. But..." I paused wondering if I should share more. She looked at me. Her eyes shining with a gentle invitation to speak. "Lately, I feel like I want to be held."

I began to tell Anne about the feelings, and the emotions intensified--the flush beneath my skin that opened every pore with a starvation for a mother's touch. An embrace that cradled me close to a breast. Soft round arms blanketing me in a thick fragrance of love and protection.

"Did your mother ever hold you?" Anne asked.

"No, but that was my fault. She says she tried to give me affection, but I wouldn't accept it. I always pushed her away."

"Do you have any idea why?"

"No, I just remember I was angry with her and was always trying to prove that I didn't need her. I guess I'm starting to regret that now. My body aches to be held like a child, but it's a little late to be mothered."

There was a deep sadness in Anne's eyes. Either she felt the same pain, or she felt mine so deeply she could show me what it looked like.

"Dawn, I hear you blaming yourself for this. Wasn't anybody responsible for you?"

"Yes, they were, but like I said, I made the decision to raise myself. I didn't want anybody's help, and I guess in a way, my behavior caused me to be neglected."

"Behavior doesn't cause our neglect," she said. "Neglect causes our behavior, and for you to make a decision at such a young age to be so totally independent, you had to somehow come to the conclusion that you were taking better care of yourself than anybody else in the house."

"Anne, I'm responsible for my own life. I don't want to dump this back on my parents."

"It's not necessary to dump it back on them. In fact, you don't ever have to talk to them about it. But for your own welfare, you need to become aware of what was their neglect and what was yours, and right now all I'm hearing is that, from the time you were just a little kid, you felt so powerful that you could push away the adults in your life who were supposed to care for you. And now that your childhood needs have surfaced, it's all your fault."

"That's what it feels like."

"How old is Jen?"

"She's almost 5-years-old."

"If Jen was not getting her basic needs met, would you blame it on her?"

"No."

"Then you should have some compassion for yourself, because in essence, you are no different than your children."

No different from my children? I was completely different from my children. They were innocent, joyful, untainted by the world. I couldn't remember a time when I felt the same.

"Trust me on this," she said. "The unresolved past is in the present trying to be healed. Caring for your children might be bringing up what your experience was like at their age."

"And, I have to feel this?"

"How we feel leads us to our callings. It opens the way to new experiences."

"This calling feels more significant than how I feel."

"I'm sure it is, but that's the path we need to take."

I looked at the small clock on a side table as Anne stood up to walk me to the door.

"Is it all right if I hug you?" she asked.

I smiled, flattered that she'd asked, more comfortable with the request than I would have thought. She held me until I pulled away. More than a brief moment and I would have felt awkward.

"I don't know what your plans are," she said, "but by some leap of faith you've come here. It's up to you if you want to follow it." Her words were spoken through her eyes, a stare I didn't break. I thought about Jeff giving me her card. How many weeks it had survived in the back of my minivan wadded up on the floor. But there was something incongruent about her. When she stood, her shoulders moved down instead of back, as if she thought she was smaller than she was. I wasn't sure if I could fully trust her, but I knew I needed help, so I committed to weekly sessions.

CHAPTER THREE

I tried to go back to work twice that month. I never got as far as the car. My desire to grow the company or start a new one, thoughts that usually energized me, now left me motionless with fatigue. The only thing I felt was a deepening depression and the insistent pull that somehow told me there was a reason for all of this.

My struggles paralleled Jeff's escalating frustrations. He would call during the day to ask me when I was coming in to work, while I counted the hours to my next therapy appointment. In the afternoons, he would bring reports home that he said needed my attention before he headed down to the beach with one or more of the kids. While they were gone, I would review the reports. Numbers that once drew vivid pictures of market position and financial condition, now looked like blurred ink on a one-dimensional page.

Before dinner, they would return with a stick, a bird feather, or a worn lobster buoy that had floated in from one of the fisherman's traps. The kids would place their new treasures in the yard while Isabella kept me focused enough in the kitchen to not burn the quesadillas or Mac and Cheese we were cooking.

Looking for a fast track out of my deepening depression, I increased my sessions to twice, sometimes three times, a week. Yet, every time Anne hugged me good-bye, an embrace that was lasting a little longer each session, my despair seemed to worsen.

"You know," I said as I set down my keys and plopped down on the couch, "ever since I started to see you, my symptoms have gotten worse."

"What symptoms are you referring to?" she asked as she took her seat.

"This sense that I'm receiving a spiritual summons is still relentless. The need to be held by a woman is more desperate, and I now constantly feel like I'm about to be killed."

Anne leaned forward as she looked at me, her dark-green silk blouse draped loosely over her leggings. "When you say you feel like you're about to be killed, how do you experience that feeling?"

"With terror, a kind of hopeless panic. When I've had this feeling in the past, I associated it to my health and thought I was dying from some fatal disease. But now I feel it every day. It's as if the fear is coming closer."

"Do you recall when it started?"

"It goes back as far as I can remember...maybe to when I was five or six years old."

"Did you ever tell your mother about it?"

"Yes, several times. But she told me I worried too much and suggested that I take up an art project or a musical instrument."

She shook her head and let out a deep sigh, then leaned back in her chair and thought for a moment. "Have you ever heard of guided meditation?"

"No."

"It's a technique used for achieving a state of focused concentration. It allows for more of the unconscious mind to come forward into conscious awareness."

"How do you do it?"

"You just close your eyes and take a few deep breaths. With your eyes closed, your mind will begin to focus inward, and the breathing will help to keep you relaxed."

"Will I remain conscious?"

"Yes. You will be conscious the entire time and you will always have control over your experience."

"Okay. If I'm in control, I'll give it a try."

I leaned back on the couch and closed my eyes. Anne began to speak in a slightly lower pitch, a peaceful tone that made me feel almost safe. She asked me to take a few deep breaths and to release any muscle tension in my body.

"When you're ready, I want you to ask a child to appear, and when the child appears, I want you to describe it to me."

I thought the exercise was ridiculous, but, after a few more breaths an image of me as a child appeared in my mind. "I see her. It's me when I'm about five."

"Describe her to me."

"I'm wearing jeans and a black turtleneck. My hair is blonde, about shoulder length, with long bangs pushed to the side and my face is smudged with dirt."

"What else do you notice about her?"

"Her eyes. She looks intense... perceptive. Not like a child... but like she has already grown up."

"Ask her if it's all right if we speak with her for a few minutes."

The image was strong. I could feel the intensity of my concentration on the child. With my thoughts I asked if she would speak with me. Without any conscious attempt on my part, the image of me as a child answered, *Are you my mother?*

"Anne, she wants to know if I'm her mother."

"Tell her for now you will be."

Before I could respond, the child said, *I don't trust you*, and ran into the darkness.

"I lost her, Anne. She said 'I don't trust you' and then she ran away."

"She's just a child. Go get her."

After a few seconds the child, with an intense gaze and a furrowed brow, returned.

"Dawn, who doesn't she trust--you or me?"

'Both of you.' She turned and ran away. I tried to get her back, but this time I couldn't. I opened my eyes feeling worse than when I walked in.

"This child is inside of me?"

"Yes, she is and she needs you right now."

I shook my head. "I hate this," I said.

"What do you hate?"

"I hate these feelings of abandonment. It's like I'm an orphan in a prison camp and those feelings just don't coincide with my life."

Her eyes touched me like a gentle hand.

"I think that five-year old can tell us a lot about those feelings."

"So what do I do next?"

"Keep working with the five-year-old. See if she will let you hold her. That younger part of you is real and she needs your love right now as much as your children at home do."

"Okay, but I'm confused why she's looking for a mother. I had a mother."

"That's all right. I'm sure when she trusts you, she'll let you know."

I looked over Anne's shoulder to the clock on the windowsill. Our hour was almost over, and as safe I was beginning to feel with her, it felt better to close the session before she did. I stood and picked up my keys. Anne confirmed our next appointment and opened her arms. I smiled and walked into her embrace. She pulled me in snug against the warmth of her soft body, and instead of holding my breath until I pulled away, I stayed in her arms and let go of a breath I had been holding forever.

Angie, the office manager, called that week. Jeff told her to hire a warehouse manager that she knew wasn't right for the job. She asked me to intervene. As much as I didn't want to get involved, I also knew Jeff tended to make snap decisions just to get my attention, and I was a bit concerned this was one of them. I made a call to the recruiter and to a few of the other employees that interviewed the young man he wanted to hire. Angie was right. The background check on the potential employee would have put the company at risk, but Jeff wanted to hire him anyway, mainly because the young man liked to fish, and Jeff was always looking for new fishing buddies.

I put the kids down for a nap and I walked out to the patio and called Jeff. He answered on the second ring.

"I think I know what this is about," he said.

"Then you probably know that I don't think it's a good idea to hire that candidate for the warehouse."

"Oh, does that mean you are coming back to work now?"

"No, I'm not coming back."

"Then why are you calling me about this?"

"Because I'm still the CEO of the company and I need you to run it for me right now."

"Then I'll run it the way I want to," he said as he hung up the phone.

I slowly put down the receiver. Jeff wore a tie like a noose. He told me from the time we began the company that he was there to support me, but he did not want to be in charge. If he had his way, he would spend his days on a fishing boat, and I was starting to fear, that one way another, that was the direction he was heading.

That night I heard him come through the garage door later than he usually did. I was watching *Sesame Street* with the kids when he walked into the family room. He glared at me.

"I need to talk with you," he said.

"Okay." I handed the remote control to Jen and walked into the small loft I used as an office that was tucked away in the corner of the upstairs. He sat in the chair behind my desk. I took a seat on the daybed that was pushed up against a window that looked out into the yard.

"If you are not coming back to work," he said, "I want you to step down as CEO and give me the position." I stared at him in silence as his words echoed in my mind. He began to raise his voice. "And I don't want you to come in, or call employees, or go to lunch with our accountant or our customers. If I'm going to be in charge of the company, then I want to be completely in charge."

My chest tightened and I suddenly found it difficult to breath. The thought of losing control of the company, not having contact with employees, or an option to return, sent a deep chill of panic up my spin.

"You decide," he said as he stood up to leave. "Come back to the company part-time or make me CEO."

I slept in the loft that night. Tossing and turning wondering if I could truly stay out of the business. Wondering if I really trusted Jeff enough to run it. I wrestled with my options until my chest flared, reminding me that I had a calling to answer. Going back to the company was no longer an option.

The next morning at breakfast, I relinquished my title to Jeff. The air that left my body that day seemed to enter his. Pride filled his large barrel chest as he put on a navy-blue suit and left early for work. I stared out the kitchen window as he pulled out of the driveway.

"It's okay, Dawn," Isabella said. "It's okay."

I nodded. "Sí, Isabella. I hope so."

After giving up my position, the depression worsened, and the internal pull intensified. My body was flooding with feelings that didn't make sense and I began to feel like a walking zombie. That winter, the doctor's office called to tell me that I missed Katie's 18-months-old checkup. I forgot to sign a release form so Matthew could attend a library field trip with his pre-school class. A week later, I forgot it was my turn to run the carpool and Jen and her best friend were in tears as they entered school 30 minutes late. I hated myself for disappointing the kids and was starting to feel as worthless as the toast I was burning.

While Jeff took over the business, Isabella and Laura were my saving grace at home. Laura and I had been best friends and neighbors since Jen was born and she was trying to catch the balls for me as quickly as I was dropping them. She boldly entered the kitchen one morning, her long dark hair pulled back in a ponytail, wearing a pair of colorful leggings and an oversized college sweatshirt she claimed covered the 30 pounds of baby weight she could never seem to lose.

I was writing a list when she walked in. Jen's birthday was just a few weeks away and I was doing all I possibly could to pull myself together long enough to give her a much-needed party.

"What are you doing?"

I looked down at my list. The only word on it was cake.

"Losing my mind," I said.

"What's going on?"

"Therapy is driving me crazy."

"Ahh and I thought Jeff would have driven you crazy first."

I smirked at her.

"How do you like her?"

"Who?"

"Your therapist."

I turned away and poured Laura a cup of coffee. My feelings for Anne were becoming so strong I wasn't sure how to describe them.

"She's good," I said, "I'm starting to feel safe with her, which makes me nervous, if that makes any sense."

"You are letting down your guard."

"I didn't know I had a guard."

"You're kidding, right?"

"I wish I was," I said as I poured myself a cup. "But it's been months and I still don't understand what this is all about. I guess that takes time."

"How's Jeff doing?"

"He's annoyed. But so far we're managing it."

"Do you think he's afraid you're going to leave him?"

I thought for a moment. I couldn't imagine Jeff would be afraid I would leave. We had been together since we were 16-years old and if he knew anything about me, he knew I was loyal.

"I think at this point he just wants me to feel good again. And I want that too. Whatever this is, it's brutal."

"I've been depressed before. It doesn't last forever."

"How did you get out of it?"

"Meds. Nothing like a good happy pill to turn your life around."

"Yeah. I think I need to figure out what this is all about first. Honestly, this depression seems like it's only a stage in a greater change I'm going through."

"It's a journey," she said.

"It sure is."

"Well, I'm here for you," she said as she hugged me goodbye.

When Laura left, I went upstairs to the loft with my journal, sat at the desk and closed my eyes. Within a few moments, the image of myself as a five-year old appeared. She was sitting on the cement curb across from my childhood home. Her nose was peeling from sunburn and her feet were leathery from refusing to wear shoes. I asked her questions, but she didn't answer. Then I imagined taking her in my arms. When I did, her thoughts became mine. I felt like a little girl trapped in a pitch-black alley, my back against the wall, my breathing so shallow it had almost stopped. Killers lurked around me listening for my voice; my silence and the darkness were my only protection. As I held her in my arms, my thoughts unraveled into babbling phrases.

They're going to kill me!

The image disappeared as a terror rose in my body so quickly I thought I was going to lose my mind. I called Anne and told her what was happening. She sounded concerned and asked me to come in that afternoon.

Anne embraced me as soon as I walked into her office.

"Are you okay?" she asked as I sat down on the couch.

"This feels so crazy."

"Do you remember anything or anyone who could have threatened your life?"

"I've been thinking about it all day. The only thing I can remember is a man who once tried to lure me into his car."

Anne's eyes grew larger. "Why didn't you tell me this before?"

"It was nothing. I was riding my scooter in front of my house and this man stopped at the street corner and asked me my name. By the time I got within a hundred feet of his car, I knew the guy was a kidnapper and I turned around and rode away."

"How did you know he was a kidnapper?"

"I guess I just had a sense of it. He was sitting in his idling sedan, looking at me as if I were an animal he wanted to eat for dinner."

"Where did you run to?"

"I rode my scooter back to the house, grabbed my brother and sister off the front lawn and pulled them into the house."

"Do you remember anything else? Anything that happened after you ran in the house?"

"I remember locking the doors and closing the curtains. My mom kept asking me what I was doing. I didn't want to tell her because I thought it would scare her, so I just kept yelling at her to not let the kids go outside."

"Wait a minute. You didn't want to scare your mom? What about your fear?"

"I thought she'd overreact if she knew somebody had tried to kidnap me and that would have made the whole thing worse."

"Did you ever tell her?"

"A few hours later, when I was calm and I knew the danger was gone."

"Did anybody call the police?"

"Probably not. Anne, do you think this is what has me so scared?"

"I'm not sure, but if you don't mind, I'd like to do a guided meditation on the memory to see if we can get more details."

I was afraid to close my eyes. But I knew I had to keep going. I sat back in the chair and took a few deep breaths. Comforted by the music in the background and the smoky-sweet smell of her perfume in the air.

"When you're ready, I want you to go back to the day you were five-years-old and the man stopped in front of your house."

The image of his car came up immediately. "He's driving an old blue sedan with a big dent on the door. I'm riding in the street on my red scooter when he stops."

"What happens next?"

"He stares at me for a while, and then asks my name. He tells me he has something for me. I need to come into his car to see it."

"What happens next?"

"He asks me again to come up to his car and I bolt down the street on my scooter toward the house. I pull my little brother off his tricycle and then pick up my sister off the lawn." My voice started to crack. "She's so little, I'm afraid he's going to get her."

"You're okay, just stay with it and tell me what happens next."

"I'm in the house locking the doors. I'm angry and scared, and there's nobody here to help me."

"Is your mother there?"

"Yes...but...but you don't understand. There's nobody here...there's nobody here to help me!"

"Go get your mother or father. Bring in an adult who can help you."

A distant image of my parents came into my mind—my mother kneeling on the living room carpet with my father standing behind her. The image was dark as if they were in a dimly lit room, their silhouettes barely visible. I tried to focus on the image, hoping to see them more clearly, when a panic rose in my chest and suddenly my words took on a will of their own. "No. No." I yelled. "I don't want to know this! I'll die if I know this!" My body broke into a tremor as I opened my eyes and jumped to my feet. "I don't want to know this" I said as I paced around the small room. "I really don't want to know this!"

"Dawn, it's okay, you're safe. You need to keep telling yourself that. You are safe."

"No, I'm not! This is death. Something is going to kill me." I dropped down beside the couch and brought my knees to my chest covering my head with my hands.

"Dawn. I want you to breathe and to look at me." Her voice sounded calm, but urgent.

I looked into the deep blue light in her eyes. There I saw safety. I saw love. I felt myself calming down.

"Keep breathing," she said. "Your mind is dealing with something in the past; whatever it is, it has already happened. You need to keep telling yourself that." She leaned forward and the air between us felt warm, safe. I took a deep breath and released the clench in my jaw.

"Why am I so scared?"

"I don't know. I'm as confused about this as you are."

"Do you think I was abused by somebody?"

"There's no way of telling. It could have been a lot of things. You might have almost drowned in the tub when no one was looking. You could have been trapped someplace and thought you were going to die. There are so many things that a child's mind can perceive as fearful that you can't jump to any conclusions. When you're safe enough with yourself to understand what happened to you, your mind will let you know."

I ran my palms down the front of my jeans trying to dry the sweat off my hands. "Anne, I've been depressed for over 6 months. I don't know how much more of this I can stand."

She looked at me. "Can you close your eyes again?"

"You have got to be kidding me."

"No, but this time we are going to go to a safe place."

I stared at her in protest, then leaned back and closed my eyes.

"Dawn, I want you to keep breathing and remember a time when you felt safe. Wherever that is, go there now and tell me where you are."

As I focused harder, I felt slightly dizzy. Then an image of a woman wearing an orange shawl appeared in my mind. She was hovering in a sitting position with her legs crossed, and in her arms, she held a healthy, round infant. Below the woman was an image of my mother, pregnant on a delivery table. I got the sense that the image was showing me who I was before birth.

As I explained the image to Anne, my consciousness merged with the infant in the woman's arms. My hands, feet, and chest began to warm.

"What's happening to you?" Anne asked.

"I'm safe here. Wherever I am, I'm safe." Slowly the image disappeared as a thought emerged and lingered.

Anne stared at me as my eyes came into focus. "What just happened?"

"I don't know. It felt like I was a pre-born infant in the arms of a woman. But she was more like a spirit. A wise, maternal spirit." I stared through the window as I spoke. "The image looks like a painting I have over my fireplace. It's an abstract of an American Indian woman wrapped in an orange shawl with her legs crossed." I pulled up my arms and showed Anne how the woman's hands came up from under her shawl, positioned as if she were holding an infant.

"Jeff and I bought the painting at a local art fair shortly after Jen was born."

Anne smiled. "Art often represents parts of our self," she said.

"You think this woman is a part of me?" I asked.

"Yes, I do. We all have archetypal wise or sage energy in us. I think you are accessing that part of yourself."

"Then why do I feel like she is separate from me?"

"I don't think you are consciously connected to that part of you yet. But she is wanting to connect with you. Your mind is showing you that. Did you notice anything else about her?"

"A thought emerged when the image faded, to love myself." It sounded so trite when I said it out loud, but it felt so essential when I received it.

"That is a pretty powerful message."

"It felt like it was a requirement to live in that kind of peace."

She nodded. "I would have to agree."

Our session was almost over. The terror I was in when I entered her office had completely subsided. I picked up my keys and thanked Anne with a long embrace, our bodies fitting together so snugly it felt as if we were one. With everything else going on, there was also something happening between Anne and I that I wasn't sure I understood. To say it was love, felt inadequate.

When I got home it was dark. I opened the front door and followed the screams and laughter upstairs to the playroom. Peaking in, I saw Jeff sitting on the sofa with Katie in his lap while launching stuffed animals high into the air. The kids were running around the room screaming, trying to dodge the animals as they fell. Jeff continued to yell out commentary as Jen and Matthew ran into toys, each other, and the pillows on the floor that were designated as safe zones. I walked in the room.

"Mommy! Mommy!" yelled the kids as Matthew ran toward me and wrapped his body around my leg.

"How was your appointment?" Jeff asked.

"It was good."

"You look happy."

"I seem to have found a source of peace."

"Great. That's a relief," Jeff said as he stood up and handed me Katie, ready to remove himself from the noisy room.

"Where have you been, Mom?" asked Jen as she grabbed my sweater and led me onto the couch. I put my arm around her and pulled her up on my lap.

"I went to visit a friend."

"What's your friend's name?" Jen asked.

"Anne."

"Is your friend helping you?" she asked.

"Yes, Honey. I think she is."

Jen's pug nose wrinkled toward her eyes with a smile, and suddenly it felt as if I were looking into a mirror. The sight of her gentle face slightly blurred and a sadness rose in my chest. I somehow had dropped from the peaceful consciousness of the wise woman, back into the lonely, isolated feelings of the inner child.

"Can I meet your friend someday?"

"Maybe. Maybe that will happen."

"Are you excited about my birthday party?"

"I can't wait for your party, Honey." I said with a smile as I swallowed down the sadness in my chest. "It's going to be so fun."

That night I was reading *The Cat In The Hat*, to Matthew and Katie. When I realized they were asleep in my arms, I carried them to bed and then curled up with Jen. The nightlight cast a soft glow on her long, dark eyelashes as her straight blonde hair framed her round face. Her two front teeth had recently fallen out and her legs now reached to my knees.

"Jen..."

"Yeah?"

"Do you love yourself?"

"Yeah, Mom, I do."

"How do you know?"

She smiled. "Well, at night, right before I go to sleep, I think about all the people I love, and all of a sudden, I pop up. Sometimes I'm at the beginning of the list, sometimes I'm at the end, and sometimes I just pop up in the middle."

She started to giggle. "It makes me laugh every time."

"It sounds like you have a lot of love."

"I have so much it feels like I'm going to explode. Sometimes at school I just have to get rid of it, so I run up to my teacher and give her a great big hug." Her eyes twinkled. "The funny thing is, when you try to give love away, it comes right back at ya."

"I bet your teacher loves having you in her class."

"Mom, I think she loves everybody." I smiled. Jen's teacher was the kind of woman who did seem to love everybody.

I kissed her goodnight. "You'd better get some sleep now, Buddy."

Jeff was downstairs watching a soccer game with Isabella. He spoke fluent Spanish and the two of them were speaking so fast there was no way I could keep up. Too tired to join them, I crawled into our bed and turned off the light. I rolled over and hugged my pillow to my chest, then closed my eyes and thought of all the people I loved. Faces and names popped into my head, but my own was nowhere in sight.

The next morning, I called my mother. She usually came up and saw the kids once a month but since I started therapy, she seemed to come up less frequently. I'm sure the idea of me recalling my childhood to anybody, let alone a therapist, made her uncomfortable. She knew how much I hated her wine, cheese, and pass out on the couch parties as a child and I'm sure she was waiting for me to bring it up. Instead, I told her about the fear I was experiencing and asked if I had ever had a near drowning experience or anything similar that would make me feel I was going to die. There was nothing out of the ordinary that she could remember. I asked again and she became defensive.

"We did the best we could with you," she said, still drawling out her vowels from her fading southern accent.

"I'm not blaming you for anything," I said as I tightened my jaw. "I'm just looking for some information."

"Dawn, it was always hard to tell whether anything ever happened to you. When you were scared or hurt, you just got angry and pushed everybody away—and you did that a lot."

She was right; if something ever did happen to me, I wouldn't have gone to anyone for help. Least of all her. She felt more like a jealous sister than a mother to me, wielding her authority around the house like a petulant child. I hung up the phone and walked downstairs ashamed to think of what she was telling my father. She would make fun of my fears as if I was on a tangent. He would shrug in disgust thinking I had too much time on my hands, and too much money in my pockets.

I sat down on the ottoman in the living room and looked up at the painting of the woman in the orange shawl that hung over the fireplace. The energy that came from the artwork was palpable. Her body covered most of the canvas. Her large almond shaped eyes rested nearly closed as she looked down toward her longer than life fingers positioned as if she were holding an infant. The distinct and perfectly symmetrical features on her face, and the rounded shoulders that sloped into her full busted frame were oddly similar to my mother's. And although I had never thought of it before, maybe she was what I imagined my mother could have been had she evolved beyond her fears and self-interests. Soft and wise. Strong, compassionate, and loyal to the spirit of her children.

⅏

My sessions with Anne continued, as did my internal conflicts. I felt a heightened sense that I was being guided and cared for, almost like our entire house was enveloped in a cocoon. The thick intimacy that often filled the air gave me hope and reassurance, but it didn't seem to relieve my emotional yearnings. If anything, it intensified them. My desperate needs for love, affection, and security that I deemed weak, offensive, and burdensome to others were now all I seemed to be. Ashamed of how much I was beginning to need Anne, afraid that she wouldn't want to see me if she knew, I began to cover up my desperation with a veil of rational insights and complaints about Jeff that I didn't really have. For most of the session she would let me control the conversation, only occasionally breaking into my commentary with a question about how I felt about what I was sharing. I didn't give her an answer. Partly because I didn't know, and partly because I was afraid to be as vulnerable as I was feeling.

When I'd pick up my keys and leave her office, I'd return home and sit with my knees to my chest in the corner of my bedroom closet. With her perfume still lingering on my sweater, I'd curl up wishing I had the nerve to tell her that what I really needed was for her to take me home, hold me in her arms and give me a safe place to cry. A place that wouldn't end in an hour. A place where I could trust her to care for me because she wanted to, not because I paid her for it.

I didn't think I could get that kind of relationship from therapy, and I still wasn't sure why I wanted it, so I kept my desires to myself and tested her relentlessly. How quickly would she call me back if I left a message? How flexible would she be in making my appointments? And if I was going to continue to get involved in our relationship, how involved was she willing to become?

I entered our next session looking for some security while trying to cover up my need for it. I tossed down my keys on the end table and took my seat on the small couch.

"Anne, you know how you said I'm going to need to trust you?"

"That would help," she said.

"If I trust you to care for me, I would like to know you have something at stake."

She looked puzzled. "Help me understand what you need."

"I'm really not interested in going to the depths of my soul while you sit behind some wall of authority and take notes about it. If I'm going to have an emotional investment in this relationship, I want you to have one too."

"I already do."

"You do?"

"Yes. I do." She said in a soft soothing voice that seemed to come straight from her heart. "But, there are therapeutic guidelines, boundaries I need to set for your protection."

"My protection? I can take care of myself."

"I don't think you understand the dynamics involved in therapy. You could become very vulnerable here, even dependent."

Dependent. I couldn't stand to hear the word.

"I'm not going to get dependent. I've never needed anyone, and I have no intention of starting."

"For a while, you might need to depend on me. You might need to trust that I can support you while you let go of the strong hold you have on yourself. I want you to know that it is all right to let me care for you."

I shook my head. "No, it isn't. Anne, you have a life outside of this office. A life that could take you out of here at any time."

"You're right, I do have a life. But part of my life is my job, and right now that job is to take care of you and help you through this depression."

"Why do you care if I get through it?"

"Because you're worth caring for, and I fully intend to do so for as long as you need me. You can trust me, Dawn, I'm not going anywhere."

I wanted to believe her, but I didn't.

"I don't need anybody to take care of me, I just need to be understood. Ever since I was a little girl, I fantasized about having somebody come into my life and see right through me--see how scared I am and give me the love, acceptance, and understanding that I need."

"We all want that."

"We do?"

"Sure. I think there is a deep yearning for wholeness and understanding in every human being, but I don't think you're going to find it from somebody else."

I rolled my eyes.

"Dawn, I believe that's what that child is trying to tell you. You need to find your own self-love and compassion. And when you learn how to love, accept and understand yourself, you will be able to share that with others."

"Anne, I don't believe in that bullshit that I'm my own hero. I've spent my entire life being there for me, and I'll tell you, it's lonely and unfulfilling."

"I think if you really look at your life you might find that you have been protecting yourself from your thoughts, not trying to understand where they came from or who you really are. You may think it's bullshit, but we can only receive love to the extent that we can love ourselves."

"Well, that might be how it is, but it still feels like if the right person knew how to love me the pain would finally go away."

"Dawn, I'll give you what I can, but you need to remember something very important about our relationship."

"What's that?"

"The hunger and yearning you feel to be held, and to be loved, is from the child inside of you who needs and wants a mother. That mother needs to be you. I can't fill that role."

I looked at the floor as a stab of rejection pierced through my stomach.

"I know this might sound harsh," she said, "but I'm not here to feed you. I'm here to teach you how to fish."

"Then I better learn quickly, because right now I'm starving to death."

CHAPTER FOUR

The early morning sun filtered through the palm trees as Jeff helped me take the kids car seats out of his SUV and put them into the minivan.

"Want to trade?" he asked as he lifted out the seat. "You can go to work and fire the technician who was shipping computer parts to himself, and I'll take the kids to the harbor."

I looked into his eyes, noticing how handsome he was in his freshly pressed white shirt and red tie. "I wish I could," I said. "I'd be happy to fire that guy."

He fastened the seat in the minivan while I reached behind him to put in the stroller. "Just out of curiosity," he said with a hint of sarcasm. "Are we ever going to have sex again?"

I looked at him and smiled, a part of me wanting to give him the passion he needed, while another desired to keep him at arms distance, frightened that his needs would somehow consume me. "I'm sure we will someday," I said as I leaned towards him and kissed him goodbye.

Laura met us at the harbor along with Cynthia, another neighbor that I had met at a few Bunko games. Her husband, Brad, was a fishing friend of Jeff's and I wasn't sure what Jeff was sharing with his friends or what Cynthia knew. She asked if she could buy me and the kids our drinks which made me think something was up. We sat down at the outdoor tables across from the boat slips. The kids ran around a gated area while we sipped our coffee.

"How are you feeling?" Cynthia asked, "I heard you have been struggling."

I looked at Laura. She shook her head as if whatever Cynthia was talking about it wasn't coming from her.

"I'm doing okay. Just trying to figure out some things."

"We're all trying to figure out things," she said. "I've been in therapy for years."

"Years?"

"Oh yes. I love my therapist. She's the only way I can stand to stay married."

"Who do you go to?" Laura asked.

"Her name is Anne. Anne Myers. Have you heard of her?"

My stomach cringed. Somewhere in my mind, I knew Anne had other clients, but I didn't want to know about them.

"I've heard of her."

"Jeff told Brad you were seeing her too."

And there it was. I walked right into a conversation I did not want to be having.

"She's been helping me move through some depression."

"Well, if you ever need to talk about it, we should go for a walk. She has helped me so much. I know she'll be great for you."

"Thanks," I looked at Laura, "ahh I forgot, I still have to shop for Jen's birthday party. Sorry, but I need to run." I called the kids and left as quickly as I could load them back in the car. So many things felt awful about that conversation, but I was too confused to figure out what they were.

Jeff came home early that afternoon. I was coloring with Matthew when he walked into the playroom. His face was red and the muscles in his neck were protruding. With a rigid straight arm, he handed me a report. I recognized it as the company's accounts receivable statement. At the bottom of the page, a large amount due over-90-days was circled in red ink.

"How did that happen?" I asked.

"It happened because our customers aren't paying, and your employees need some direction." His forehead creased into a pleat.

"What do you want me to do about it?"

"Nothing," he said as he turned and walked out of the room. "I'll handle it like everything else around here."

I got up and followed him. I wanted to remind him that he asked me to stay out of the company. But I didn't have the energy to risk starting a fight, and I knew the accounts receivables, and his extra burdens around the house, were not what was making him angry. He needed more physical attention from me, and I continued to avoid it.

He ripped off his tie and pulled a beer from the refrigerator.

"I'm sorry about work," I said. "Do you want me to call our banker and extend the line of credit until we receive payment on the receivables?"

His shoulders began to let down. "That would help," he said.

"Okay. I'll take care of it today."

"Thank you. I'm going to the beach."

He unbuttoned his shirt and walked out of the room as Isabella walked in.

"Jeff no happy?"

"Si, no happy con work, no happy con me."

"Necesario más cerveza," she said with a smile.

"Possibly me más cerveza," I said.

"Si. Yo tambien."

I went to the loft, called the bank, and got our line of credit extended.

Jeff returned a few hours later with a lobster buoy in one hand and an empty beer cooler in the other. He appeared much lighter. I wish I could have felt the same.

My struggle between pride and insecurity continued to rage in my head, as I sat in the lobby of Anne's office. My feelings for her continued to confuse me. More than ever, I needed to trust that she cared for me, but her skillful techniques to maintain our therapeutic relationship, and her genuine personal feelings for me were becoming harder and harder to distinguish.

"Dawn, come on back."

I looked up from my chair and saw Anne. When our eyes met, a warm smile came to my face.

We sat down and she handed me a small note.

"What's this?" I asked.

"It's my home number. You can always reach me there."

My heart continued to warm. "Thank you. I promise I will only use it if I have a gun to my head."

"Promise me you will use it way before then."

"Deal."

"How are you feeling?"

I thought for a moment. "The same. But this is really getting difficult for Jeff. I think I might need to go back to work."

"There is no reason you can't go back."

"The only reason is my body won't let me. I literally can't move in that direction."

"Then maybe you should ask the universe for help."

"What do you mean?"

"I think we get what we need if we ask for it. Maybe you should ask for some relief for Jeff or for the issues he is having at work."

I looked at her and nodded, "Jeff will be relieved when I feel better so let's move through this."

"You want to go back to your childhood home?"

"No. But like you said, whatever it is, it already happened."

"You have a lot of courage."

"Actually, I'm just too scared to stay still."

"Okay, then, when you're ready, close your eyes and take a few deep breaths."

The piano solo playing from a small stereo box on the floor of Anne's office soothed me into a flooding sensation. Anne asked me to let go of my thoughts with every breath.

"When you're ready, I want you to go back to the front of your childhood home."

I tried to focus but all I saw was black.

"Where are you?" she said. Her question brought up the image of the woman in the orange shawl in the same cross-legged sitting position. Far in the background of my mind, I saw a small bright light that looked like a distant star.

"The woman is here... and so is a light that looks very far away." I opened my eyes for a moment and looked around the room for an overhead lamp that might be causing the image, but the room was dim with diffused light. I closed my eyes again and a few moments later the image re-appeared.

"This is really strange, but there's a light in my head."

"What does the light want?"

"It wants to talk to me... it wants me to come closer. Anne, this is scaring me. I don't want to go near the light."

"It's all right. You can stay right where you are. Does the woman scare you?"

"No."

"Ask her what you need to do to help yourself."

"Trust." The word rolled off my tongue. "She told me to trust myself."

Shortly after, the image of me as a five-year old appeared. Behind the child was a man I couldn't distinguish. My mouth started to water as a strong wave of nausea came over me. I opened my eyes and clenched my jaw until the sensation subsided.

"Are you okay?" Anne asked.

"Yes. I just need to stop now."

She came over to the couch and placed her warm hand across my clammy forehead.

"Are you sure you're okay?" The touch of her skin brought my mind back into focus.

"Yes. I'm okay," I said as I took a deep breath.

"What just happened?"

"I'm not sure. I keep getting this image of a man. The image is dark and faceless. I can't tell who it is." My stomach began to tremble.

"Do you get any feeling with the image?"

"I feel like something very awful is about to happen."

Anne held her soft gaze. "Remember, whatever happened already happened," she said. "It is the five-year-old who is scared, not you."

I wiped my damp palms across my jeans. "Who is this woman, Anne? And why does her image keep appearing?"

"Like I told you before, I think she represents a wise and knowing part of you." Anne went on to explain that the images I was receiving were common in therapy. That with focused concentration people can access wiser parts of themselves that can give them clarity and direction. "That's why I prefer to work with guided meditation," she said. "The information is very insightful and it's coming from you. You are always going to know what you need to encounter and when."

"What about the light?"

She slowly nodded her head. "The Light is a universal figure. It is powerful. And, apparently it wants to talk to you."

"Well, I don't want to talk to it."

"Why?"

"Because I'm scared. Because talking to a light is strange. Because it's a whole lot more powerful than I am and I don't know what that will do to me."

"Give yourself time Dawn. I think you need to move through some of these interpersonal struggles with your parents and how those relationships might have affected your self-esteem before you will be prepared for an encounter like that."

I stared past Anne through the window behind her. My heart felt congested as if I was stuck in the place just before tears.

"You look a little dazed. How do you feel?"

"Sad. Alone. I hurt all the time, and I still don't know why."

Anne's eyes filled with sadness.

"For once in my life, I just wish I could cry," I said.

"I want those tears for you."

We sat in silence for a moment. Then she picked up her pen.

"If you look at some of the feelings you have found in the inner-child work and the perceptions you have as an adult, you might find a theme in your life. Something that you perceive as continually happening to you."

"I don't know, there's so much here. I often feel somebody wants to kill me and I'm in great danger. I yearn to be held by a mother. There are feelings of abandonment, guilt, and mistrust. And yesterday, when I was taking a nap with the kids, a strong thought came to my mind. It was like a message."

"What did it say?"

"It said it was time to know the truth about my father."

"Did it mean anything to you?"

"No, it was just perplexing. I've always loved and admired my dad. He came from a poor family and became a successful architect. He is a hard worker and he taught us to be the same. I don't know what other truth there would be."

She tapped her pen for a moment, then wrote the word Love on a clipboard and handed me the paper.

"I want you to write a sentence using this word."

I scribbled out my first reaction:

Love hurts, it can't be trusted, and it always leaves.

I handed back the clipboard.

"When in your life have you experienced this?"

"Let's see...when my older brother left for college. And then a few years later when Jeff and I broke up."

"Why did you break up?"

"I found out that he was cheating on me with a waitress in the local bar."

"Ouch," Anne said. "That must have hurt."

"It almost killed me," I said. "A few months later we got back together, but emotionally I don't think I ever fully came back. I just couldn't risk that pain again."

Anne looked perplexed. "Then why did you marry him?"

"Because the thought of letting him go was too painful."

"So, when you wrote down, 'love hurts, it can't be trusted and it always leaves', that is truly how you experience love?"

"Yes, until I had Jen."

"How was that different?"

I didn't know how to explain it. My baby girl nursing at my breasts rooted me to earth like never before. And the affection that poured out of me, like she'd tapped an unknown geyser straining to be released.

"She needed to be loved," I said. "And it felt safe to love her."

"So, you're safe to experience love only if somebody's needs depend on it?"

"I guess."

Anne shook her head. "Dawn, when you get home, I want you to start writing with the sentence, 'I felt abandoned when...' and then set a timer for five minutes. Keep your pen moving the entire time, even if you start to doodle, keep writing."

"Okay, but this path I'm on seems to be getting darker." I said as I stood up to leave.

"Well, there is a light in your head, so I think whatever happens you are going to be okay."

Our hug lasted a little longer that day. The child inside of me was finally feeling safe and the love that came from her embrace was filling me as if I was a famished orphan.

I didn't have time for the writing exercise that night. With all the talk of abandonment, I thought I'd better spend some time with my husband. After dinner we put the kids to bed and went into our room for the evening.

He wasn't interested in talking about my therapy, and I wasn't interested in work, so we talked about the kids for a minute, then he leaned over to kiss me. I laid back on the down-comforter and tried to relax. The lust that filled his body with power, a desire that once stimulated me, was now repulsive. I felt guilty for denying his past attempts, so I clenched my teeth and closed my eyes. His lips pressing up against my neck suddenly felt lecherous. The dominance of his body over mine enraged me. I held my breath and tried to make him disappear, then exploded with aggression and pushed him away.

"Don't do this to me!" I lurched forward to hit him.

He grabbed my arm and held it down. "What's wrong with you?"

I looked up at him. And in the dim light, I realized it wasn't Jeff holding me down. It was my dad.

I pushed Jeff off me and ran to the bathroom. He followed me while I paced the floor.

"You're shaking," he said, "What's happening to you?"

"I think I had a flashback. It's my dad. He…he…was on top of me."

"Your Dad did this to you?"

"I don't know, Jeff. I don't know. I can't believe my dad would hurt me like that."

He grabbed a towel and put it around my shoulders. "Do you want me to call Anne?"

"No. I see her tomorrow. I'll be okay until then."

He walked me back to bed, but I was too restless to sleep. I tossed and turned all night, trying to get imagines of my father out of my head.

The next morning, Anne greeted me in her office with a long embrace. My hands were still shaking from the night before. "Are you okay?" she asked.

I told her what had happened with Jeff.

"This is so crazy but the thought that my dad hurt me keeps screaming through my mind." My voice cracked, "I'm scared, Anne, I'm really scared." My arms and legs started to tremble.

Anne sat across from me and pulled her chair close. "Whatever you're remembering is in the past. It has already happened and you're safe now."

"I don't understand this. I can't believe my dad would ever hurt me."

She watched me like a cautious mother. "We haven't talked that much about your father. I'm going to need to ask you a few questions."

I nodded as I tried to warm my hands, rubbing them up and down on my jeans

"Do you know if your father was a pornography user or whether he exercised any deviant sexual behavior?"

"I saw an occasional X-rated movie around the house, and I know he liked to go to burlesque shows in Las Vegas, but for the most part he was a very unpretentious, well-respected businessman."

Another surge of fear ran through my body and I began to tremble from head to toe.

"You're okay, Dawn, just take a few deep breaths."

"I feel sick," I said as I controlled the urge to vomit.

Anne pulled the trashcan out in front of me then softly squeezed my shoulders until I started to calm down.

"Let's see if we can move through this," she said. "Can you close your eyes?"

I took a few deep breaths. "Okay," I closed my eyes but didn't lean back.

"Unclench your hands and remember to breathe. When you're ready, go back to your childhood home and tell me what you see."

"I'm still scared."

"It's okay. You can open your eyes at any time and see that you are safe and I'm sitting right here."

I took a deep breath as a chamber in my mind began to open. I was a four-year old remembering a time when he took me into his car to play. I was wearing his favorite pink and white dress that day. I was excited, looking forward to the special time with him. We walked out to the driveway and climbed into the front seat of his red Mustang. We both started to giggle as he unzipped his pants and took both my small hands and placed them around his erect penis.

"Anne," I explained, "this is fun. I'm laughing. Dad's laughing. It's a game we play."

"How old are you?"

"I'm about four. But he's not hurting me. He loves me. I'm very special to him. It's like he is my best friend, and we are so connected. I remember, it was like he and I had our own family. Just the two of us. It was so loving."

"Tell me what else you're feeling."

"Happy, playful. I love my dad, and he loves me and we make each other happy." I opened my eyes and looked at Anne, "he was just playing a game—a game to show me how much he loved me."

Anne shook her head. Her brow pushed into the ridge of her nose. "He may not have physically harmed you, but you were being damaged. Dawn, you were four years old and he was sexualizing your love. There are a thousand messages that go with that kind of attention and none of them are healthy for a child."

A panic rose in my chest and words I couldn't control started babbling from my month. "He hurt me, he hurt me. I need to stop now. They will kill me if I keep going."

She took a deep breath. "Who is going to kill you?"

"I need to be safe," I said as I stood up and paced the floor.

"Nobody can hurt you here. You needed to be safe as a child and you weren't. But you're an adult now and now you are safe. I promise. Nobody can hurt you here."

I passed through a wave of nausea as another memory began to emerge. I sat back down and stared at the floor.

It was the summertime, just before my fifth birthday. I was lying on the couch in the family room watching Saturday morning cartoons with my brothers. Dad came in and handed me a dress to wear. It was a white dress with little purple flowers, and I didn't want to put it on. I didn't like dresses anymore. I knew what they meant and I didn't want to play.

Dad told me to get dressed and to get into the car. We were going to the store. His voice was low and angry. I didn't know what I'd done wrong, but I knew I was in trouble. After I put on the dress, I found my mom in the laundry room folding clothes. My little sister was crawling all over her. I told her I didn't want to go with Dad. With her back to me, she turned her head and snapped, 'Do what your father tells you to!' I asked her again and she yelled for my father to come get me.

I stared down at the floor. "We drove up the hill by the big white cross and then turned down a dusty dirt road that led into a canyon. He stopped the car, yanked me by the arm, and threw me down in the back seat."

"Do you know what happened after that?" she asked.

I closed my eyes and held my head. "I can hear his voice. He's calling me a bitch. He's talking to me like I'm an adult. Now he is calling me a cunt. He's a different person. This is so confusing."

"Try to stay with it." Her voice was clear, calming.

"I see him on top of me but I'm not in my body. My viewpoint is from the roof of the car, like I'm a speck on the ceiling looking down on us. I don't feel anything. I'm completely out of my body."

"Do you know what happened next?"

I opened my eyes. "He raped me."

There was a long silence then I looked up at Anne. "There was blood on the seat. It was my fault. I made the mess."

Anne's eyes looked torn between anger and tears. I felt shooting pains in my vagina as the memory continued to flow.

"I stayed in the back seat until we got home and then he took me into the bathroom with him. I cried out to my mom. He's telling me to shut up or he's going to kill me. Oh, God, he hates me so much."

Anne sat down across from me, her eyes still glazed with a tear. "You didn't deserve to be treated that way. This should never have happened to you."

I slid to the corner of the couch and pulled my knees up to my chest, nodding in silence as I continued to remember.

"I wanted him to forgive me for making him so mad. For making him do that to me. It happened right before my... my... birthday, and I... I thought maybe he would give me a present to... to show me he still loved me. But he didn't. He wouldn't talk to me. He didn't love me anymore, and it... it was my fault." I pulled my knees further into my chest and dropped my head between them.

"This was not your fault, Dawn. This was not your fault at all."

I started to slowly rock trying to keep myself intact.

"How do you feel right now?"

"Like, I'm a 5-year-old who just lost her parents."

"Dawn, I need you to look at me. You are not alone. I'm here and you survived it."

I glanced at her for a moment and then tucked my head back into my knees. I was so riddled with shame that I couldn't keep eye contact.

"What's going on right now?"

"I... I... I don't have me anymore. I... I... don't know who I am."

She came over to the couch and put her arms around me softly rocking me while the present moment continued to collapse into the past.

"I'm sorry," she said. "I'm so sorry this happened to you."

The feelings of being brutally punished and discarded by my parents was so extreme a breaker switch went off in my mind that disconnected me from my body. Suddenly I couldn't feel my skin, my legs, not even the air I was breathing.

"I... d... d... did such a bad thing."

"No you didn't. You were 5 years old. This should have never happened to you. Please look at me," she said. But I couldn't make eye contact. I felt so worthless and empty I just wanted to die. She rocked me slowly, reminding me to breathe. When I could feel my legs again, I slid them back to the floor as she held me close to her chest.

"I couldn't see myself in the mirror anymore," I said. "I didn't know who I was."

"Ah. That's why you were looking into the mirror." She tightened her grip around my shoulders. "Abuse takes away our natural identity," she said. "You were probably trying to get that back."

I sat up and started to shake my hand hard, as if to expel something from my body.

"Are you okay?"

"Yes... I... I... I'll be okay."

"Here, have some water."

I drank the glass, then walked around the room.

"How are you feeling?"

"Like the script of my life has suddenly been re-written."

"It hasn't been re-written. You're just safe enough to finally read it."

"I was raped by my father." I said it over and over--in disbelief, in confusion, in a state of shock. I remembered the brutality of his words, his belt on the floor of the car, and painful body sensations, but after my first reaction all I felt was shame. A sense of filth in my body that encompassed me.

"I'm not telling anybody about this," I said as I sat in a daze.

"You might change your mind about that."

But I swore in those hours I'd never tell a soul. The truth about my father would hurt too many people, and I didn't want to be the cause of their pain.

"This is not your fault." Anne repeated the sentence a dozen times, but her words felt meaningless. Everything about the memory felt like I was to blame. I had betrayed my mother by being with my father in a way that I knew wasn't right. And, I betrayed my father by asking my mother for help. The confusion in my young world was so overwhelming it was impossible to see my innocence.

The rain poured down on the bay window and the light of the day had dimmed to dusk. Anne wouldn't let me leave until she knew Jeff was home. He was in Los Angeles for the day and with the rains he could be in traffic for hours.

"I can't talk about this anymore today." I said.

"Then what would you like to talk about."

"Let's talk about you."

She smiled. "What would you like to know?"

"Do therapists have better marriages than the rest of us?"

"Not necessarily. We have our stuff too."

"Like what kind of stuff?"

"My fears and abandonment wounds come up in relationships like everybody else's."

"You have abandonment wounds."

"Yes. To some extent, I think we all do."

We sat in silence for the next several minutes. The events of the day, and the open-ended time frame had brought us to the intimacy felt by old friends sitting up by a late-night fire. The comfort was so thick, the closeness so intense, neither one of us wanted to leave.

"I could stay here forever," I said, "but I should really go home."

"Is Jeff home from work yet?"

"I'm sure he is home by now."

The world outside looked dark and cold, and what I really wanted was to crawl up in her arms for the rest of the evening. Stay with the one person that finally made me feel safe. I picked up my keys.

"I wish I could stay with you," I said as we embraced.

"I wish you could, too," she said as she held me tightly.

CHAPTER FIVE

Katie had almost finished her glass of wine. I had barely touched mine.

"Mom, she was really crossing some boundaries with you."

"I think she did cross some boundaries. But what later happened between us was something I can't judge. It really was beyond our humanness."

"Did Dad know how you felt about her?"

"He did. But it didn't seem to bother him. She was so tender with me, and I was so broken. I think he was relieved that she was helping me."

Katie's phone pinged and she looked down to read a text.

"It's Jen," she said. "Her and Matthew are on their way over."

"Great. But let's not talk about this when she's here. It was a difficult time in our lives. I just want to focus on her wedding."

"That's fine. She only wants to talk about her wedding anyway."

She turned over her phone. "Dad must have wanted to kill your father."

"He did. But that wouldn't have solved anything. He took his frustrations out on a punching bag for a while, then he just started smoking pot."

"Can't blame him for that."

"No, not at all."

"Dad does have good weed."

"I wouldn't know. He never smoked it around me."

The door flew open and Jen bounced in with a box more than half the size of her body. She was almost six foot tall with Jeff's blue eyes and milky skin that still freckled in the sun.

"My wedding dress is here!"

Matthew slipped off his size 12 shoes and walked in the door behind her. Sliding across the wood floors in his socks, singing, "And Matthew is here, too."

"Put it on," Katie said.

"I'd love to see it," I said as I stood up and gave them both a hug.

"Nice hair, sis," Matthew said to Katie.

Katie ran her hands through her long-tangled hair that had frizzed around her face from working in the garden.

"It's beauteous," she said.

I ordered a pizza and Matthew helped me make a salad while Katie and Jen went into the bedroom and put on her dress. A few minutes later she emerged, sparkling as bright as the diamond on her finger.

"Do you love it?"

Tears welled in my eyes, dripping down my face before I could catch them.

"You are stunning."

"You don't think it's too tight?"

"No. It fits you perfectly."

She came up and hugged me. "You're not going to cry through the wedding are you?"

"Only when I first see you walk down the aisle."

She walked back and forth in front of the mirror while Matthew snapped his fingers and danced around her.

"Has anybody heard from Dad?" she said as she went into the bedroom to take off her dress.

"There was an outbreak of the virus in southern Texas," Katie said. "He was having trouble getting a flight out."

"He texted me about an hour ago," Matthew said. "He got on a plane."

"That's a relief. I can't wait to see him," said Katie.

"Do you want to go with us to the airport?" Matthew asked Katie.

Katie looked at me and sat down. "No, I think I'm going to finish helping Mom."

Matthew quickly ate a plate of salad and kissed me goodbye.

"Mom, remember we're meeting the wedding planner at 10 a.m. tomorrow," Jen said.

"Yes. I'll be there."

"You better set an alarm or something. You can't be late."

"I'll be on time."

"Ok, but don't forget."

She picked up her keys and the two of them hurried out the door, barely closing it behind them.

"Why does she do that," Katie said, "you're hardly ever late for anything."

"I know. I think she still has PTSD from the balls I dropped during that time in my life."

"So, what happened next, and what did the Light want with you?"

"It wanted to communicate with me. That part of the story is what I think is happening now."

"Then it wasn't about sexual abuse?"

"That was my path, but it led to something much more universal. I had to move through those interpersonal memories and emotions first before I could open up to the greater experience."

"Then what did it say?"

"Don't worry, we will get there."

"Okay," she said as she sat back in the chair. "Then what happened after you remembered the abuse? Did you tell Grandma?"

"I did, and at first it was validating."

❧

Jen's 5th birthday party was that March, the Saturday after I remembered the abuse, and despite the feeling that I was falling apart I was trying to keep myself together for the day. I only told Laura and Jeff about the abuse. I didn't want to get my parents involved until after the party. I was struggling enough to track the details of entertaining ten 5-year-old children for the afternoon.

"Party time," Laura said as she showed up with a handful of helium balloons and a box full of small gift baskets for the children. She put down the gifts and gave me a hug.

"How are you holding up?"

"With a large cup of black coffee and a handful of chocolate chips."

"That ought to get you through."

Isabella and I finished making the sandwiches while Laura put the candles on the cake and Jeff hung up a pinata. Shortly after, the doorbell rang. Jen ran through the house with Matthew and Katie trailing behind her.

"It's Grandma! It's Grandma. She's here!"

Laura looked at me. "Are you ready for this?"

"I've played along for 33 years, what's another day."

My mother walked into the kitchen with a big smile and a hand full of presents. Her olive skin and dark short hair looking radiant next to her bright yellow pants suit. She knelt and the kids pulled the gifts from her hands one by one.

"How are you?" she asked as she walked over and gave me a hug. Not a full body hug like Anne would give me, but a one handed, barely touching around my shoulder, followed by a quick squeeze and release.

"Come on Grandma," Jen said as she pulled her by the hand into the living room. "Can we open the presents?" Katie and Matthew yelled as they were jumping in place. The whole scene would have been priceless had it not been tainted by unlocked memories.

The kids all arrived. Jeff's childlike nature kept everybody entertained and Jen beamed with delight through the afternoon while I pushed down the memories of what was happening to me at that age.

"Are you going to say something to her?" Laura asked as she stared at my mom blowing bubbles with the kids.

"I think I need to ask her what she remembered first," I said. "Let's see how late she stays."

By 5:00 most of the children had been picked up. Jeff was outside drinking a beer and our kids were falling asleep one by one in front of the television. My mother helped clean up the last of the cake plates with Isabella, then packed up her things and started walking toward the door.

"Before you go, do you have a moment?" I asked.

"Sure. What do you need?"

I helped her load her things in the car and then we took a walk down the street.

My hands started to tremble, so I pushed them in my pocket.

"Mom, are you sure you don't remember anything unusual about my childhood? Any events that stood out as strange?"

"Dawn, I've told you. You were an independent kid. You did things your own way, and whenever I tried to help you, you just pushed me away."

"That's because I was sexually abused." The words seemed to just pop out of my mouth.

She didn't respond, and she didn't ask by whom. Everything in my body felt numb as we kept walking.

"When Dad took me with him on Saturday's he would molest me. And one day he got mad and raped me."

We both stopped. She turned and looked at me, her brow creased in disbelief.

"That's impossible," she said. " Your father would never do that to you, and children that young are too small to be raped."

Her ignorance never ceased to amaze me. "Children are not too small to be raped. Are you sure you don't remember anything that would have been a sign of sexual abuse?"

"No, Dawn," she said as she shook her head. "You always liked your father."

"Do you remember how I use to leave with him alone, to go to the store or to his office?"

"Yes, but you two did that all the time."

"Do you remember what I was like when I came home? If I ever looked scared or hurt?"

Her eyes glazed over, as if she were going into a trance. After a long pause she started to speak in a tone that sounded as though she were thinking out loud.

"There was one day... and you would have been around 5-years-old. You were in the bathroom with your dad. I heard you crying from down the hall. I went up to the door and asked if you were all right and you screamed to me that Dad had hurt you. He yelled back that you just fell off the counter and he was handling it. So I walked away." Her finger pointed like she was talking to the air. "But I remember what you had on that day. It was a white dress with little purple flowers."

Oh, God, she remembered it, too. The father I created in my mind, the one who would never hurt me, was gone. Dead. "Had we just come from the store?"

"Yes, I think it was a Saturday morning... you two had just gone somewhere."

"Mom, I remember that dress, that day, and that was the day I remembered being raped by Dad in the car. Right before he took me into the bathroom."

She snapped out of her daze. "Dawn, that's crazy. I've been married to your father for thirty-eight years. He could never do anything like that."

"I know it's crazy, but it's true. It's the memory I didn't want to know about."

"I can't believe this," she said.

"I don't want to believe it either, but don't you think it's strange that twenty-eight years later you can remember what I had on that day? Mom, I can't tell you what my kids had on yesterday. You knew something was wrong. You knew."

"I did know something was up with you two that day." She paused for a moment, her eyebrows creased toward her nose as if the truth about my father was starting to creep into her consciousness, then she shook her head and glared at me.

"Dawn, your father could never have done that. And even if he did, sexual abuse wasn't public knowledge like it is today. We would never have known what to look for."

"I know Mom, but it happened. I think you should come in and see my therapist with me."

"No, no, that's not necessary. I'll go home and talk to your father about this."

We walked back to the house talking about my behavior as a child. The way I pushed her away. The hard exterior I developed so young and the need to contain and control my emotions. When we reached her car, she looked at me. "It's hard to believe that your father could do that to you, but I believe you. You have my 100 percent support," she said as she used both arms to hug me goodbye.

A wave of tension lifted from my body. I was cautiously optimistic that she would finally understand me. Perhaps support me as an adult, if not as a child.

After the kids went to bed, Jeff and I went in the backyard and laid down in the hammock. When I first told him about the abuse, he was so enraged at my father he had to leave the room. The birthday party was the first time I had seen him smile all week.

The garden fountain trickled as the moon began to light up the cool night. I shared the conversation I had with my mother while he sipped his glass of gin.

"You think she's really going to help you? I know she's great with the kids, but I've never seen her be very nurturing to you."

"She validated the memory. That made me feel a little less crazy about all of this."

"What a sick man," he said. "Honestly it's taking every ounce of self-control not to take my shotgun and go off that fucker."

"Then I would just lose you, too."

He set down his drink on the lawn and pulled me closer into his arms. I had always felt safe in Jeff's embrace, like curling up to a big bear that I knew would protect me from harm.

"I can't believe that I could just block out those memories and have no recall until now."

"You have to block that shit out," he said. "I can't remember the entire year my dad died. When I look at pictures of me at that age, all I remember is how pissed I was that he left me with two sisters and my mother."

"At least your mom adored you."

"She hardly adored me."

"Are you kidding. The woman wouldn't say hello to me the first two years we were dating. She just sneered at me like I was stealing her baby boy. Remember that time in high school when I climbed out of your second story window just to avoid seeing her when I left your house."

He started to laugh. "I remember that she was standing in the patio when you landed next to her rose bushes."

"Oh my God, talk about a scary parent."

"My dad was the nice one," he said.

"I wish I would have met him."

"I wish you would have met him, too. At least we would still have one good father left."

My head started to hurt.

"I guess this explains why you were so damn tough as a kid," Jeff said. "When I first met you, I thought you were going to kick my ass."

"When I first met you, we were the same size."

"Hey, I was an inch taller."

"Your hair was an inch longer, I'm pretty sure we were the same height."

He scoffed and pulled a throw blanket from the end of the hammock and wrapped it around our shoulders.

"Maybe we should get away," he said, "we could go to the cabin in Mexico. And, on the way... I can stop by your parent's house and kill your father."

I wrapped my legs around his and tucked closer into his chest.

Jeff and my dad had always been friendly. Hearing his anger made me further realize, the relationships in my family were all about to change.

"Do you think remembering the abuse is what this calling has been all about?"

"No. It feels like I have to release these memories to find out what it's about."

"So, what do we do now?"

"I think I just have to continue to follow the path."

He looked up at the sky. "I know I'm supposed to support you through this. And, I will. But I have to tell you, it's getting harder."

"I know, I know."

🎗

The following week, I was making breakfast for the kids when there was a loud knock at the door. Matthew and Jen went running toward it. They could see from the window it was my neighbor, Cynthia, and the door was half-way open by the time I got there. She stood in the entry with a loaf of freshly baked banana bread and a book. I handed Jen the bread and the kids ran back to the kitchen. I stood speechless looking at the title, *The Art of Forgiveness.*

"Don't you just love Anne," she said. "She suggested this book to me a few months ago and I thought maybe you could use it. It really makes life so much better."

I wanted to slam the door on her. She's got to be kidding me. I looked down at the title again wondering what Cynthia knew and how she knew it. Or, if she was just trying to be friendly and her timing was deplorable.

"Thank you," I said. "I'm sorry, I have to run. The kids are eating." I closed the door while she was still speaking and walked back to the kitchen. I tossed the book in a cabinet and put the bread in the freezer.

"What's wrong, Mom?" Jen asked.

Her voice made me calm down. "I'm just a little frustrated."

"You love banana bread. Don't you want some?"

"I do. I guess I'm just not in the mood for it. But if you would like some, I can pull it out and cut you a slice.

"No, I'm not in the mood for it either."

I had an appointment with Anne that afternoon. I walked in perturbed and handed her the book Cynthia had dropped off that morning.

"I have a very nosy neighbor and apparently she is also one of your clients. She said you recommended this book to her."

She slowly nodded. "You know when you work in a small community like this people are bound to know one another."

"Well, I hate to admit this," I said, "but it kind of bugs me that I know another one of your clients. And why would she give me this book right now? It seems so inappropriate."

Anne shook her head. "I'm sorry you had that experience. But I assure you, I never discuss my clients with anyone, and there is no way I would recommend this book to you right now."

"Good because I found it beyond annoying."

"You are right to be annoyed. I'd be furious. You can't possibly forgive somebody who has harmed you until you fully experience the emotions caused by the abuse. If you tried to forgive your father now, you would just be stuffing all those feelings down even deeper." She seemed more upset by it than I was and it took her a minute to calm herself down.

"Forgiveness has its merits," she said, "but not if it's used to avoid your problems or deny your feelings."

Her eyes took on the preoccupied look she had when she was carefully contemplating her words.

"I hate it when you do that," I said. "Just say what's on your mind."

She took a deep breath. "Dawn, part of what I believe is happening to you is that your consciousness is expanding.

You are connecting to a deeper, wiser part of your being. It's an awakening process that changes your cellular structure and it opens your mind to new dimensions of your psyche. It seems to be happening to more people these days and the energy you are starting to release needs to be managed. Things could get worse before they get better."

"Is that why I'm remembering the sexual abuse?"

"I believe so. In order to evolve into higher levels of consciousness, your mind begins to release all the old memories, emotions and thought patterns that have kept you stuck in smaller, narrower states of awareness. It's a difficult process, but I promise you, if you stick with it, it will be worth it."

"It doesn't feel like I have a choice."

"To tell you the truth, you probably don't. It does seem like this is leading you to some kind of encounter."

"Is there anything I can do to make this smoother," I asked?

"You're getting your own guidance, and you have received good internal messages. The key is to trust them."

"Anne, it's hard for me to trust anything, let alone my own thoughts and perceptions."

"Of course it is. Your trust was brutally violated as a child, and your present world reflects your childhood. It's going to take time to correct old perceptions."

My brain felt like it was being re-formatted. "This is all so disorienting. I feel like I've landed in Oz."

Anne smiled. "Actually, that's a pretty good analogy for this kind of transformation."

"Have you done this work before?" I asked.

She thought for a moment. "I'd have to say I'm still on the yellow brick road."

I nodded and she quickly changed the subject.

"What's happening with your parents?"

I told her my encounters with my mother were sadly predictable. The day I told her about the abuse memories, I had her '100 percent support.' By the end of the week, I had false memories, a popular theory she latched onto when my father found a magazine with a cover story about a therapist who was accused of leading patients to believe they were abused by their parents.

Anne shook her head. "You know I would be happy to have them come join us in therapy."

"I know. I've asked them to come to therapy and discuss what's happening. They refused."

"Have you spoken to your father?"

"No, according to my mother he said he had a daughter for 33 years and now that daughter's gone. Apparently, I'm dead to him."

"Just like that?"

"Just like that."

"How does that make you feel?"

"Like, I'm an absolute piece of crap."

She winced. "You know this was his fault not yours."

"I wish I did know that. But it feels like I'm the one ruining our family."

"You need to keep telling yourself that this is all happening because of his actions. To heal, you have to place the responsibility on the right person. You were the child. He was the parent. This was not your fault."

Her words didn't register. The news of this was coming from me. It would destroy the illusion that we were a happy family. That my father was a good man. It was not something my brother and sister wanted to know. And, they would blame me for telling them.

❧

The school year was about to end, and Jeff called one morning and asked me to drive up to the office. He had left a file by the bed, and he needed it for an afternoon meeting. I threw on a sweatshirt and jeans and headed to the office. I figured if I didn't dress the part, maybe I could trick my body and make it inside the building.

I walked quietly past the receptionist hoping she wouldn't notice me. I got halfway up the stairs to the executive offices before I ran into our office manager, Angie.

"Dawn, how are you?" she asked, as she gave me a friendly hug. "When are you coming back?"

"I don't know. It might be a while."

Feeling too vulnerable to maintain eye contact, I looked down at the carpet and noticed a light tire-track of mud going up the stairs. I reached down and brushed at the dirt.

"What's this?"

Angie started to laugh. "Last Friday after the barbeque, Jeff drove Thomas' motorcycle upstairs into the accounting office. It was pretty funny." I looked at her and slowly shook my head. "Dawn, he's having a hard time. I think he just needed to blow off some steam."

"I want you to call me if things get out of hand around here," I said.

"Okay," she said as the moment softened. "Dawn, I never thought I would say this, but everybody here really wants you to come back."

I smiled at her. I knew what she meant. It wasn't as fun when I was there, but things were under control and Jeff was less prone to sophomoric pranks.

I darted into my old office. The blinds were shut, and the air was cold. I flipped on the light to find everything as I left it. The files on the side of my desk, a week's worth of *Wall Street Journals* stacked behind my chair, and the awards on the wall that once defined me, now hanging with a layer of dust clouding the engraved words.

"You made it in," Jeff said as he walked into the office and kissed me.

"Yes, I did. And I don't remember there being tire tracks on the stairs."

"I have no idea where those came from," he said as he cleared his throat.

I handed him the employee file he left at home and sat down in my high-back desk chair.

"You look good in that chair," he said. "Maybe you would feel better if you came back to work one day a week."

I looked at my desk and for the first time, I felt no desire to return.

"I know you never wanted to run the company, but I don't think I'm going to come back. I'm more certain than ever that I have something else to do."

"Is that something else going to include me?"

"I hope so. So far we've made a good team."

"I don't know how much longer I can stand running this place. It's seriously getting in the way of my fishing."

"I know, but one of us needs to be making money. I'm sorry, but right now it needs to be you."

"Ok, but the minute we are profitable again, I'm going to buy a boat."

"Sounds like the perfect goal."

※

Anne and I continued to meet twice a week. She rarely booked clients after my session, so if I wanted to stay a little longer I could. When I told her I still yearned to be held she would come over to the couch, pull me gently into her arms and hold me. Sometimes we just rested in each other arms, saying nothing, while I absorbed, like a hungry child, the safety I felt in her embrace.

I felt more secure when I was with Anne, but elsewhere there was little stability. California was sliding into an economic recession, and our clients were dropping as fast as my relatives.

Jeff came home one night late for dinner, with gin on his breath and a forced smile on his face.

"Where have you been?" I asked as I tied up my robe and pulled the leftover lasagna out of the oven.

"Does it matter?"

"Yes. It matters," I said as I gave him his plate. "How was work?"

"Great. Everything is great."

"How's the accounting department doing?"

"Great. We have budgeted for a new BBQ for the party this Friday."

"Sounds good."

"Yep. Everything is going great."

Jeff passed out on the couch shortly after dinner and I went into the loft and modemed into the accounting system. I pulled up the most recent income statement. When I reached the bottom line, my heart skipped a beat. The company was as depressed as I was, and I didn't have the strength to do anything about it. I turned off the computer and sat back in my chair.

"What's next, God?"

A week later, I wished I hadn't asked.

CHAPTER SIX

I tucked the kids into bed and went into our room. Jeff was reading as I went in to wash my face. We hadn't spoken much that week--sometimes it was too painful to even make eye contact.

I crawled into bed but stayed on my side.

"Are you tired?" he asked.

"Exhausted."

He put down his book and turned off the light. I rolled toward the window and let my mind wind down from the day. It was Thursday night. I usually saw Anne on Thursdays, but it was Memorial Day weekend and she and her husband had left early for a vacation to Oregon. I hoped she was enjoying herself. The work we were doing was grueling, and I was glad that at least one of us could get away from it for the weekend. Thinking of her, I nodded off quickly.

Let her go.

My eyes shot open. I sat up in bed and shook my head. No, it's just my imagination. I lay down again and closed my eyes.

Let her go.

My heart began to race. I jumped out of bed and started pacing the floor.

"Let her go," I said out loud. "Why do I have to let her go?"

"What's going on?" Jeff asked.

I turned on the light and sat down beside him.

"I just got a message. It was about Anne. She's going somewhere and I'm supposed to let her go."

It was hard to know what Jeff was thinking at that point. He didn't understand my relationship with Anne any more than I did, let alone the inaudible messages I was receiving and how accurate they were becoming.

"Has she ever said anything about going anywhere?"

"No, she's never mentioned a thing. We had an agreement. She said she was going to see me through this. I can't believe she would leave. It doesn't make sense."

"Maybe it's not true." He turned off the light and asked me to get back in bed. But I was too unnerved to sleep. I went into the loft and lay down on the day bed. Anne was restless. I had seen it in her eyes. Southern California just wasn't her style. Maybe she went to Oregon to look for a new home?

I spent the next hour calming myself down. If she was moving, that would take time. She'd have to sell her house and close her business. That would take at least a year. By then I'd be better. A year from now, I wouldn't need her the way I did today.

Tuesday morning, I walked into my session. Anne was sitting in her chair, silent, wearing the green leggings and the long, silk, leopard print shirt she had worn so many times before. I set my keys down and stood in front of the couch, a feeling of sadness hung thick in the air as our eyes met and we locked into a stare.

"Are you moving to Oregon?"

She got up and closed the door. "Can you sit down? I have something to tell you."

The blood rushed to my stomach, my knees felt weak as I sank onto the couch.

"I'm not moving to Oregon, but I am leaving. Some personal issues have come up in my life, and I can't avoid them anymore. I'll be taking an indefinite sabbatical starting September 1st."

"What?" September that was less than 2 months away.

"Dawn, it's so hard to explain this, but my feet feel like they are being pulled right out from underneath me. I've been fighting it for a while now, and I can't avoid it anymore." She took a deep breath. "In September, my husband and I are going camping in Mexico for several months. Then we plan to travel through the States for a year or two."

"You're kidding me?"

"No, I'm not. We decided this weekend. You're the first person I've told."

I stared at her in disbelief, my head spinning so fast all I could do was nod. I picked up my keys and stood up to leave.

"Please don't go," she said.

I glared at her and walked out the door. The floor down the hall felt as though it was tilting to the left. My ears were ringing so loud I thought my head would explode. Indefinite leave. Mexico! There would be no phones, no mailboxes. In September, she'd be as good as dead to me.

I leaned up against a wall and pressed my hands against my throbbing temples. Where was I going? Anne was the only one who knew how painful this was. My mind went blank for a moment, and then I turned around and stormed back into her office. The door was open--she hadn't moved from her chair.

"How can you do this to me!" I slammed the door behind me. "You promised you would be here for me! You promised you would help me through this! It was our deal, your commitment to my healing. How the hell can you walk out on that?"

I picked up the rubber door stop and threw it at the wall.

"You asked me to trust you, and I did! You told me it was safe to depend on you, and I do! You told me you would be here for me and now you're not! Are you really so fuck-ing selfish that you're willing to re-inflict me with the same wound I grew up with!" I wanted my words to cut her, to stab her deeply so she would bleed as badly as I was bleeding.

She looked down at the floor and collapsed into tears. "I'm so sorry."

My anger disappeared as I watched her cry. She looked so hurt, so vulnerable. All I wanted to do was hold her.

Let her go.

Oh, God, that's right. I dropped my forehead into my hands. She did have to leave, and I had to let her. I kneeled down in front of her chair and put my arms around her shoulders.

"I'm so sorry. I don't understand this, Anne, but I know you're doing the right thing."

She put her hand up against my chest and shook her head in tears. "No, please, please don't comfort me." Her arm went limp and I wrapped my arms around her back and pulled her in closer. She released a deep breath that deflated her body, put her arms around my waist and started to sob.

"A message entered my mind a few nights ago that you were leaving and that I needed to let you go. It didn't make sense to me at first, but now I realize there are other people that need to come into my life, and there are other places that you need to go." I couldn't believe what I was saying, or the peace of mind that came with it. We opened to a loose embrace, holding each other's hands as we kept an eye con-tact that felt soft and loving—a connection I didn't know I could maintain with anyone other than my children.

"Dawn, this was one of the hardest decisions I've ever had to make. I love you very much, and I don't want to hurt you."

We fell into another embrace. "I love you, too."

My voice came from the center of my body. The sound of my own words stunned me, the tone much deeper than I had ever heard. I let go of my thoughts and absorbed the moment. How relieved my chest felt against the warmth of her body, as if I had finally connected to what I had lost—made whole again by a spirit that enveloped us like a cocoon. She squeezed me tighter, and suddenly my focus was drawn to my center, where I felt something I hadn't felt before. From within me, yet beyond me, there arose a bubble of energy, as if the warmth that had surrounded us had entered my body--resurrecting my soul--igniting it like a small flame.

"I've never felt this before," I said.

"I haven't felt it for a long time," she told me.

I wondered if we felt the same thing. What was happening to me felt like a new life had emerged inside my body. What was happening to Anne must have happened to her before.

We barely spoke for the rest of the session. She came over to the couch and held me. I curled up in her arms wondering how I would survive this without her.

I drove home without any memory of doing so, confused about my session, knowing only that Anne's sabbatical wasn't what I was confused about. When I pulled into the driveway, Isabella was leaving for the weekend, and Jeff was packing the car for Mexico. The trip had been planned for months, but under the circumstances of the morning I had completely forgotten. Laura came over a few minutes later to stay with the children. I threw together a bag and went to hug the kids goodbye. I never liked leaving them, even for a night, but they loved Laura and as soon as they saw her they ran off with her to play in the back yard.

Jeff and I drove the next three hours in silence. He put on a pair of headphones. I stared out the window to the Mexican waters trying to untangle my confusion.

She really did love me. When her walls were down, when the boundaries were gone, I could feel how much I meant to her. But why? I hadn't done anything to earn her love. I didn't excel at a job that would command her respect. I hadn't even performed an act of sex to earn her affection. And she still loved me?

The emerging revelation was making me dizzy. The thought that someone could love me not for what I did, or what they needed, but for who I was, had never before occurred to me.

We pulled off the coast road to a white sand path that led to a one-bedroom trailer decorated with hanging shells and fishing buoys. Jeff's father passed away when he was 8-years-old and a family friend had been taking him to the trailer ever since.

Jeff handed me the keys to a padlock to open the door while he walked around the back to put a small aluminum fishing boat in the water.

I grabbed my bag and unlocked the door. Inside was an old brown rug that smelt of sun-dried seaweed. The bedroom had a window that looked out to the bay and the walls were covered with his father's oil paintings. A homage to ducks in the northern hemisphere.

Jeff had been taking me to the trailer since high school. Back then it was our oasis, a love nest away from our friends and family. I hadn't been there since the kids were born and the once quaint little home now felt dilapidated and cold.

Jeff spent most of the weekend out on the bay fishing. I stared at the ocean during the day, the stars at night.

"You're starting to scare me," Jeff said one night by the fire. "You're acting like you're brain dead."

"I'm sorry. I just have too much on my mind." He didn't ask about what.

"Anne's leaving her practice," I said. "She is going on an indefinite sabbatical next month."

"What?" he scoffed.

"She told me this morning. Remember the message I got the other night that I had to let her go. Well, it's true. She's leaving the country."

He shook his head and gulped down his beer. "I want to talk to her," he said.

"What are you going to say?"

"That I want to kill your fuckin' father. And while I'm taking care of work and the kids, I need her to take care of you." He crushed the can between his hands and tossed it onto the sand.

"I think she and I will be able to work this out."

"And who is going to help me work it out?"

"Maybe you should find a therapist?"

"We can only afford to have one of us in therapy and right now that needs to be you."

"I'm trying to get better as soon as I can," I said. "Believe me, I want this whole thing to go away as much as you do."

"Well, you better tell the masters of the universe to speed it up. I want the person I married back."

He left the fire and walked down to the water. I crawled into my sleeping bag and stared at the wall. I was no longer the person he married. And now, I was in love with somebody else. Yet, I didn't see Anne as a threat to my marriage. On the contrary, my greatest hope was that somehow the love I felt for her would open my heart, so I could bring those feelings back to Jeff.

Therapy with Anne was not the same after that. I was waiting for her to scrap our therapeutic relationship and move on to a friendship so we could stay in contact, but she didn't seem to have the same idea. We talked about her leaving and she'd slip into intimacy, her voice would soften, her gaze more loving. She would then abruptly pull back into her role. 'How does that make you feel?' was now thrown in rather than asked. 'What does that look like?' sounded contrived.

After a few sessions of waiting for Anne to make amends for our broken contract, I decided to take the initiative.

"Anne," I said as I sat down on the couch, "I support your decision to leave, but my whole being is telling me our relationship isn't over. I know that sounds like I'm dependent, and I am, but I truly think this strong feeling is coming from a deeper part of my mind."

She looked at me softly. "It feels premature to me, too, but I still have to go."

"I know you do, but can't we convert our relationship to something else? Some kind of arrangement so we can stay in contact?"

"You can't convert a therapeutic relationship to something else."

"How come?"

"It's against the law. If I'm not your therapist, I can't have any contact with you for at least two years."

"That's ridiculous."

"I know you have a hard time with this, but there is a natural imbalance of power here. The law is set up to protect you, and I support it. I've seen too many people abused when therapeutic relationships are socialized."

"I don't want to socialize our relationship. I just want to stay in contact with you."

She shook her head and pressed herself back in her chair. "I can't, Dawn. You're the kind of person that goes soul-to-soul with people and... I... I just can't give you that kind of relationship."

"You already have."

She looked away and folded her arms, then looked at me again. The light in her eyes had faded away. "I don't know how I can make you understand this, but the therapeutic boundaries really are for your protection. It's the most unselfish thing I can possibly do for you."

"Unselfish? The therapeutic boundaries are giving you a clear-cut way out of this relationship, and I'm stuck carrying the baggage."

"I'm not looking for a way out. In fact, if I had my way, I'd be taking you with me. But that's not in your best interest, and what's in your best interest is my first priority."

"If it was your first priority, you wouldn't be leaving."

I felt like I was being strapped into a straight-jacket. "Boundaries or not, this relationship of ours is happening on several different levels and it needs to run its course. If I could stop the energy behind it, I would, but I can't. It's bigger than me."

"I hear what you're saying, and I trust your feelings, but I also know what I have to do."

I stared into the corner. Was she pushing me away because she cared too much? Or, because she didn't care as much as I thought?

"Then give me a referral for a new therapist. I don't want to do this any longer."

There was a long silence, then she stood up from her chair and handed me a card. "I have been giving this a lot of thought," she said. "There's a woman who works out of the office next door. She is the therapist that the therapists go to, and she has a great deal of experience counseling people going through these kinds of transitions. I think her personality would work well with yours."

I looked down at the card, it read, Judith Edwards, M.F.C.C. Her office phone was in the lower left corner. Her home phone was on the right.

"She puts her home phone number on her business cards?"

"I think you will find Judith is very available for her clients."

I picked up my keys from the table and stood tall in front of her.

"Do you want to set up our next appointment?" she asked.

I stared at her with disdain. "No. I'll call you."

Her eyes welled with tears as I reached for the door. "Dawn, I know it's hard for you to believe anything I say right now, but please know there's nothing in the world I would like more than to grieve this loss with you."

I turned back and looked at her. My heart wanted to collapse in her arms, but my pride was back in control. I turned and walked out the door.

When I came home, Matthew and Katie were sitting in front of the TV and Jen was reading a book to Isabella. Everybody looked like they needed some fresh air so I gave Isabella a break and walked the kids up the street to the park. They ran off to the jungle gym while I sat on the edge of the sandbox, my teeth still grinding from the session. I could hear her words. 'You go soul-to-soul with people, and I can't give you that kind of relationship.' I wanted to scream. I wanted to cry. I wanted to push Anne Myers out of my life and prove to her I was never going to need her again.

Laura, wearing one of her oversized sweatshirts, walked up with her son. She rolled sunscreen over his face and he ran off to play with the kids.

"You look like one sad dog," she said. "What's going on?"

"My therapist is leaving."

"What! No way. I don't think they can do that."

"Well, they can, and mine is."

"Wow, you really care about her. That must suck."

"You have no idea how much. I can't even see straight anymore."

"Mom!" Oh, God, the kids. There's Jen...Matthew. Where's Katie?

"Jen, where's Katie!" Laura and I jumped up and ran in different directions trying to find her. I went around the playground, frantic, searching for my two-year-old. Moments of terror passed until I rounded the corner and saw the edge of her red hair. I looked under the slide and there she was playing in the sand. I caught my breath and reached for her. I have to stop thinking about Anne. This relationship is driving me crazy.

Memories continue to push up from the floorboards of my mind. The nights were plagued with thoughts of my father coming into my room. I'd recall his touch then my body would go numb. When I closed my eyes all I would see is fog. Then the white light would appear, beckoning me, seemingly getting closer every time I released another memory. At one point, I knew I would have to encounter it, whether Anne was in town or not, so I made my first appointment with Judith. I figured if she was the therapist that the therapists saw, she would be able to handle me.

Judith walked out of her office just as I entered the lobby, and when our eyes met, a bolt of thunder from a summer storm rattled the building. I stepped back and looked at her.

"Do you always introduce yourself with thunder?" I asked.

She laughed. "I was about to ask you the same thing."

We continued to joke as she led me back into the small room that was adjacent to Anne's. I looked at Anne's door as I passed, feeling like an abandoned child seeking foster care.

Judith's office was more formal than Anne's. There was a neoclassical loveseat against one wall and a white floor to ceiling bookshelf across the other. Judith had the same classic look as her office. A tall, slender woman in her late 50's with fine, China-doll skin and thick, black hair that curled to her shoulders. I handed her the patient information form she mailed me after we made the appointment and took a seat.

She skimmed over the paper and confirmed the names of my husband and children then set down the form.

"So, I hear you are getting the double whammy," she said.

"The double whammy?"

"Anne tells me you are recalling abuse memories from your childhood. And now your therapist is leaving. That has to be difficult."

"I suppose it is." I glazed over the part about Anne leaving and gave her my matter-of-fact rendition of the abuse. She absorbed more than listened. Her focus was wise, not intense.

"Repressed memories seem to be only half of my problem," I said.

"What's the other half?"

"Do you believe people receive callings?"

"Yes, I do."

"Good, because I am receiving one. And I don't much care for it."

"How do you experience it?"

I explained how it all started and the internal messages I was receiving that were giving me directions.

"Tell me more about the messages."

"They are thoughts that pop into my mind without any conscious thinking. They tell me what to do next, and they seem to be leading me to do something that feels very significant."

She nodded.

"Does that sound strange to you?" I asked.

"No. We all receive messages--some people are just more tuned into them than others. Do you get them often?"

"As often as I need them."

"Do they come with images?"

"Sometimes. In my mind I see the image of a woman in an orange shawl who Anne thinks represents my wiser self or inner sage. And more recently an image of a light has been appearing." I wanted to cry. My fear of the light, and the shame that I wasn't worthy enough to know such a power, collided together like waves do in a storm.

"Sounds like very powerful images."

"They feel like it," I said. "Do you have other clients who receive messages from images?"

"Yes. Images are the mind's way of communicating the different parts of our being. They can represent parts of us that are benevolent, strong, gentle, young, old, wise, angry, or hurt. If we interact with the images, we can find out more about who we are."

"You make it sound like we're all multiple personalities."

"We are." She unwrapped a piece of candy and placed it in her mouth. "On one end of the spectrum is the person who loses consciousness as they go in and out of the different parts of their being. On the other end is someone like the Dali Lama who has brought all the different aspects of the mind into conscious awareness."

"I can understand the woman being a part of me. But I don't think the Light is."

"The Light is universal. It's inside of all of us."

"Well, it's summoning me to do something and that is kind of freaking me out."

"Any idea what it wants you to do?"

"No, it just seems significant. And it feels like I'm going to have to release these abuse memories in order to find out what it wants."

"That makes sense. But you will also have to release the feelings, not just the memories. The feelings are what keep us stuck in difficult patterns."

She asked me what had been coming up for me and I told her I was experiencing flashbacks. Just the night before, I felt like I was in my childhood room, I had a sense of my father's presence and a wave of terror came over me that was so powerful I couldn't move. It took me a few moments to orient myself to the present.

"Have you heard of post-traumatic stress disorder?" she asked.

"I know it's common in war veterans."

"It's also common in adults who have suffered from child abuse. The shock of the trauma is postponed until the survivor is in a safe enough place to process the information."

"Maybe I'm safe, and maybe I'm crazy."

"Post-traumatic stress can make you feel like you're crazy, but you're not. Your mind is trying to heal from the past, and I believe the night terror you're experiencing is trying to tell you something, trying to help you heal. Have you written about it?"

"I do a written dialogue with myself as a child. She's been telling me there's more, but I don't believe her."

"Why don't you believe her?"

"Because I don't want to. It's too much to take on right now."

She nodded. "You would not be telling yourself about additional abuse if it was too much to take on right now. Your mind is telling you that you can handle this."

I sank into my chair.

"Dawn, when you remembered your father coming in your room, what did you see, and how did you feel?"

"I feel his energy overpower me. It was like this dark, ominous force had come to suck the life out of me. Then I can't remember."

"You dissociate."

"I feel a sinking disappointment, and then I go numb."

She sat up in her chair. "The disappointment you describe with your father's abuse, do you feel a similar disappointment when you think about Anne leaving?"

"No. Why?"

"Because your father, as your parent, had a responsibility to take care of you, to protect you, and to support you emotionally. Don't you think that Anne, as your therapist, committed to a similar agreement?"

"Anne isn't hurting me intentionally."

"No, she's not, but the situation is re-abusing you."

I didn't acknowledge her.

"Dawn, what if this was happening to Jen? What if she had been raped by the one person she loved more than anybody in the world? Kept it a secret from herself and everybody else and then finally, thirty years later, had the courage to love and trust somebody enough to help her. Then that person broke their commitment and decided to leave."

"It would be unbearable to think of that ever happening to Jen, but I'm not Jen."

"What's the difference?"

"She's just a little girl, innocent, precious."

"And you're not?"

"Judith, I was never like Jen. I was a rebellious, mischievous kid."

"You sound like you think you deserved what happened to you."

"I know it's not logical to think that way, but I still feel guilty. Like I've done this horrible thing to my mom by being with my dad."

"Your father did a horrible thing to you and your mother. And your mother wasn't much better for not protecting you."

"I still feel guilt. It's just who I am."

"Who you are is guilt?"

"Yes... I mean no... I don't know." I was pulling my hair out from the roots. "I need some help."

"I'm here to help you."

"I think I need Anne's help. She understands me."

"Anne's leaving next month and it's going to be important that you feel safe with another therapist before she leaves the country."

I looked down at the floor. I wasn't going to feel safe with another therapist. Not now, and maybe not ever.

"Have you had your final session with Anne?"

"No."

"That might be a good idea."

I stood up to leave. "I'm not ready to do that yet."

"Then go at your own pace. But she is leaving soon and you really should have closure before she goes."

I left Judith's office. When she closed the door behind me, I slid a note under Anne's door asking for an appointment.

❧

I received a call that week from Angie, our office manager. Jeff had renewed a big account which stabilized the company, but nobody knew what was stabilizing Jeff.

"I think he's finally lost it," Angie said on the phone.

I put down my sandwich and sat down at the kitchen table. "What did he do?"

"Louis, the warehouse guy, kept messing up on his paperwork, so today Jeff went downstairs and chain-sawed his desk in half."

"He did what?"

Angie started to laugh, but I knew she wasn't kidding. "He took a chain-saw and cut his desk in half. It was a joke. Everybody but Louis was in on it."

"Let me talk to him."

Angie put me on hold. It was five minutes before Jeff picked up the line.

"You probably just called to tell me how much you love me," he said.

"That's exactly right, until I heard you chain-sawed Louis' desk in half."

"It's a metal desk. I only chain-sawed through the keyboard."

"What the hell are you thinking? We could get sued for that! Not to mention that the Labor Board might have something to say about it."

"About what?"

"Management by power tools doesn't sound like a very safe method."

"Yeah, but I bet Louis won't make that mistake again."

"This isn't funny."

"A lot of things aren't funny," he said.

I took a deep breath. If I knew anything about Jeff, it was that he never asked for my help. He just resorted to something outlandish to get my attention.

"Jeff, you're under a lot of pressure. I know you don't want to go into therapy, but maybe you should reconsider it."

"Sorry, I don't have time to indulge myself in therapy. I have a company and three kids to take care of."

I could feel myself start to snap. "You think I want to be going through this?" I yelled. "Believe me, I'd much rather be at work chain sawing people's desks in half instead of dealing with the time bomb I've got going off in my head. I didn't ask for this Jeff."

"Neither did I."

There was a long pause while I took a few deep breaths.

"Will you do me a favor," I asked.

"Anything for you, princess." He couldn't have been more sarcastic.

"Bring home the financial statements and let's talk about selling the company."

Jeff came home early that afternoon, with the chain saw, a six-pack of beer and a printout of the financial statements. He drank the beer while we went through the numbers. The renewed accounts were keeping the company afloat, but the recession had our receivables out so far, we weren't going to make payroll. We needed time to sell the company and a miracle to keep us in business until then.

"Can you ask the masters of the universe to take the heat off." he said.

"I'll see what I can do."

"Good because I'm heading to the beach. And I better find a lobster buoy today."

I gave him a puzzled look as he stood up and left the room.

I was starting to believe that we do get what we need, even if what we need isn't a comfort. So, I prayed that night for some relief. I didn't think it would help but then again, stranger things were happening.

At eleven o'clock the next morning my realtor called. I owned a rental property in San Diego with my dad. He had gifted his half to me after Katie was born and a few months later I had put it on the market. It had been listed for over a year, and my realtor was calling to tell me I had just received an offer. I couldn't believe what I was hearing. The offer was good, the escrow would be short, and the equity would be enough to take the edge off--and then some.

🎵

Anne and I made an appointment that week. The morning of our session, I woke into a premonition about her travels. I had a dense, almost chaotic vision of her in Mexico and with it came a chilling sense of danger. She was going in the wrong direction, and for some reason I was supposed to tell her.

A few hours later Anne and I met in her office. When our eyes met my heart skipped a beat and I couldn't remember why I ever left angry.

I took my seat on the couch and told her about the intuition. She looked interested but not concerned.

"Considering my psychological state," I said, "I'd take any information coming from me with a grain of salt, but the feelings wouldn't go away until I agreed to tell you."

She smiled. "I trust your instincts, but I'm still going to Mexico."

"Good. I like Mexico. I think you should go. And to tell you the truth I wish whoever was giving me your information would dial direct. I have enough problems of my own to deal with."

She laughed. "Which problems are you dealing with?"

"Well, I can get strong feelings about your travel plans, but I can't connect to my emotions about the abuse. All I feel is depression, a lot of frustration and guilt."

"Those are feelings."

"But they're not going anywhere. I'm just stuck in them."

"The grieving you've been doing for the past year is about your unfelt emotions from your childhood," she said.

"If you felt all the feelings associated with sexual abuse at once, it would kill you. That's why you blocked them out in the first place."

"But I'm not a child anymore. I want to feel the pain and cry the tears, and I want to do it with you while you're still here."

She nodded. "Where did you say you feel the block?"

"It's in my chest. It's the size of home plate."

"We could try to go into the block in your chest and release it through another guided meditation."

"Whatever it takes," I said.

"Okay, but before we start, let's talk about you and me for a moment."

"Is this going to hurt?" I asked.

"I hope not. I've been thinking about our relationship and how we can maintain it."

I sat up in my chair.

"Dawn, I realize you and I are having an unusual connection that is going beyond us as individuals. However, I believe we find what we need in this world, and you found me as your therapist. I have to respect that there is a reason for that. I can stay in touch with you after I leave, but for your safety, it has to be under therapeutic guidelines."

"What does that mean?"

"For the first couple of months, I'm going to be out of the country. When I come back I'll give you a call, and if you need to see me we'll work something out."

The inside of my body felt like it was being squeezed by a giant hand, but I didn't feel I had a choice. "I will agree, but only if you own your therapeutic guidelines as your boundaries. They are not mine. They do not govern me, and I don't believe they are in my best interest."

"Okay. I agree that they are my boundaries, and we see this differently."

I smiled as a small piece of me seemed to come home to roost that day.

"Good, then let's do another guided meditation."

I sat back on the couch and closed my eyes. After a few deep breaths I began to relax into the black fog I saw in my mind. When I felt my muscles release and my body began to float, I asked for the woman to appear. The fog cleared to a light background and in the center of my mind was an image of her, sitting cross-legged with an orange shawl around her shoulders. Above her and slightly to the right was a brilliant twinkling light. The same light that once looked like a far-away star now appeared the size of a full moon.

"She's here," I said. "And the Light is back."

"Okay. Take a moment to greet them."

I greeted them in my mind. There was no response from the woman, but throughout my body, I could feel the Light beckoning to me.

"The Light still wants to talk to me."

My fear began to fog the image. The thought of communicating with such a powerful entity sent a wave of anxiety up my spine so I focused on the woman.

"The Light's gone now," I told Anne, "It's just the woman."

"Ask the woman, or the Light if it comes back, if they can help you to relieve the guilt."

The image of the woman had already disappeared, and two side-by-side pictures appeared in the center of my mind. The first image was of Jen wearing the pink and white seersucker dress I made for her the summer I was pregnant with Katie. The next was a scene from my childhood where I was playing and laughing as a three-year-old, rolling on a green lawn in a clean white dress. My focus went to the image of me as a child and a thought entered my head:

> *You were, and have always been, as innocent as*
> *a child.*

I repeated the message to Anne
"This wasn't my fault," I said. "I was just a child."

I let out a deep breath and slipped into deeper state of relaxation. Then suddenly, my head and body swooned, and a rush of energy, knowledge that came in a cluster of red, blue and gold light, flashed into my mind.

"We don't really know who people are." The words had a will of their own, as if the information had burst through a spiritual dimension and was now coming out of my mouth. "Anne, this is about you." I repeated the information as I received it. "We don't really know who people are. When I see your soul, I'll see my own." My mind went dark and my body fell into exhaustion. I took a few deep breaths and realized what I had said. My eyes shot open and I stared at Anne. She looked stunned. "I swear I didn't make that up."

"I know you didn't," she said.

I sat up and tried to orient myself to the room, rubbing the skin of my arms, trying to get a sense of my body. Then I looked back at Anne, knowing her eyes had never left mine, comforted by her accepting nod.

"When I see your soul, I'll see my own. Do you know what that means?" I asked.

"No, but I trust it. I had a strong feeling we were going to get something important today."

I looked around. Her office suddenly felt like a cage. My path appeared to rely on my relationship with her. It could take a lifetime to see my soul in hers and, as much as I loved her, I didn't want to need her one day longer than I had to.

"Did you understand the message about your innocence?" she asked.

"Yes, that was clear."

"Good. What is important for you to understand is that the abuse was not your fault. You didn't deserve it. It was your father's sickness, not yours."

"I understand that, but this other information has taken me by surprise. I need to go home and think about it."

"I need to think about a few things, too," she said.

Anne came over and hugged me goodbye. "This is going to be okay," she said in our lingering embrace. "Really it is."

I picked up my keys and we set up an appointment for the following week. When I left her office, I ran into Judith. She looked at me and slowly nodded.

"I'm going to make another appointment with you," I said, "I'm just wrapping up some loose ends with Anne."

"I understand, and I really think it's important that you have closure soon. You are going to need to be able to trust that somebody else can help you before Anne leaves."

"I'm okay. Anne and I are going to stay in touch when she's gone."

"You and Anne can do whatever you want. But for our therapeutic relationship to be effective, you need to have closure. The relationship you have had with Anne is over and that needs to be acknowledged."

I forced a smile, told her I'd call her, and walked out of the building.

When I pulled into the driveway, Jeff was hanging a 100-pound punching bag from a rafter in the garage while Jen and Matthew were drawing on the sidewalk with pink and blue chalk. The kids dropped their chalk and ran up to the car. I opened the door and bent down to pick up Matthew when Jen put her arms around my neck.

"Mom, are you feeling good today?" Jen asked.

I looked into her bright blue eyes. I wasn't only feeling good, I was feeling innocent. As innocent as she was.

"Yes, honey, I'm feeling very good today."

"Then come swimming with us. Pleeeeeease..."

"Okay, go put on your suits."

They ran into the house and I walked up and kissed Jeff.

"What's the punching bag for?"

"To keep me from killing your father. Here try it." He put a pair of boxing gloves on my hands and held the bag from behind. "Go ahead and hit it."

I swiped at the bag a few times.

"Fun, but I think I'd rather go to the pool with you and the kids."

"Well, that's a good sign. Did you and Anne work it out."

"I think so. We are going to stay in touch after she leaves."

"That's a relief."

"It really was."

That day there was a small break in my inner storm. Jeff and I coated the kids in sunscreen and went up to the community pool. I put our towels down on a chair while Jeff did a cannon ball plunge into the water, splashing a wave of water over the kids. They screamed with delight, and with Katie in my arms I stepped into the pool. The joy was so simple. The kids ducking under the water, and then popping up to make Katie belly laugh like a Buddha doll. Jeff putting the kids on his back, jumping in and out of the water as if he were a giant whale in an amusement park. They showed me how good they were getting with their swim strokes. Jen and Matthew's heads trying to roll side to side as they'd pop up and gasp for air.

That afternoon there was nothing in my mind but the sounds of my children's laughter. The past temporarily washed away by the cool water shimmering over my skin, the sun kissing my shoulders, and the sweet taste of fruit juice squeezed from a snack box.

CHAPTER SEVEN

For the next month, I ping-ponged between therapists. Each time I would meet with Judith she would try to get me to see that Anne leaving our therapeutic relationship was a circumstance that was re-abusing me. I listened but refused to make the connection, not wanting to taint my feeling for Anne with the horrific memories from my childhood.

I would then meet with Anne. We didn't talk about abuse memories anymore. Most of the time she just held me.

Anne called me one evening after dinner to schedule our last session together. The request seemed abrupt which made me think she and Judith had a conversation. My heart raced as she spoke. My teeth clenching together as I made the appointment and got off the phone.

"Who was that?" Jeff asked as he was putting the dishes in the washer.

"Anne. We are having our last session tomorrow."

"What are you going do then?"

"I don't know. Honestly, I don't understand why this is happening."

"That makes two of us," he said as he walked out of the kitchen and into the garage.

I showed up to her office with nothing to say. There were no choices, no words of consolation. I knew Anne had to leave, but I couldn't help but feel like I had just become a casualty in somebody else's war.

The office was locked when I arrived. I sat down on the floor, pulled my knees to my chest and leaned against the wall. Anne walked up a few minutes later in a pair of shorts and a maroon cotton shirt that accentuated the awkward way she pulled down her shoulders, her body a contrast to the gentle glow that seemed to shine up from under her skin.

"Sorry you had to wait," she said in a soft voice.

I cracked a smile and followed her in. The room was almost bare. Most of her things had been packed away and the small furnishings had been removed. I sat on the couch while she rolled her desk chair in front of me.

"Before we get started," she said, "there is something I have to tell you."

"Wait, let me tell you. You're not going to Mexico anymore, you're going someplace in Asia."

Her eyes grew wide. "I'm starting to think I should be paying you. How did you know?"

I told her a few days after our last session I awoke into the vision of her boarding a plane to Asia. The knowing didn't startle me. Either way, she was leaving, and it felt like she was now heading in the right direction. I swallowed hard as my throat started to tighten.

"Dave can't get off work right now, so I'm going to meet a friend who's traveling through Thailand. I'll be back the first of December, and then he and I are going to Mexico."

I nodded. She wasn't going to go to Mexico, but I'd let her figure that out.

She took a deep breath and settled down in her seat. "How are you doing?"

My chest was so heavy with sadness there were no words to describe it. I sat silent for a moment before I could find my words.

"I'm doing okay. Maybe just a little sad."

"I'm sad too," she said.

The air between us was thick with intimacy. So thick it made me feel like I couldn't move.

"Are you up for a quick guided meditation? I really want to help you find a safe place to go before I leave."

"Sure. That's sounds like a good idea."

"Okay, whenever you are ready."

I leaned back in my chair. After I took a few breaths, she started speaking.

"I want you to imagine a long white path. At the end of the path is a gate. You are going to walk down to the gate, and when you open it, envision yourself in a beautiful garden, a sanctuary where you can feel warm, loved, and completely safe. When you enter the garden, look around and tell me what you see. Notice the details as they appear."

The image came up as she spoke, I walked through the gate into a garden of freshly cut grass, enclosed by tall, manicured bushes that separated it from a dark surrounding forest. A small stream ran through the bottom half of the sanctuary. There was a white bench on a lawn underneath a coral tree and several budding red-rose bushes were scattered around the yard. I took a seat on the bench and the image of the woman appeared, sitting cross legged wrapped in her orange shawl. I told Anne what I saw.

"Good, go ahead and greet her," Anne said. "Then ask her if she has anything to tell you."

Words arose from my chest.

There were others.

My lungs deflated as if they had been punctured. I couldn't talk. The implication was devastating.

"Dawn. Are you okay? Tell me what you are experiencing."

I asked again and the inaudible words again rose from my chest.

"There were others."

"Do you know who the others were?" Anne asked.

I exerted my conscious control. "No, I don't want to know this."

"Okay, just relax and ask the woman what you need to do."

I took a deep breath, then above the woman, the brilliant white light appeared and I received an inaudible message.

Write the book.

I repeated the message to Anne as a panic rose in my chest.

"Write the book. Do you know what that means?" Anne asked.

"No. but I want to open my eyes now."

"Okay, but before you do, ask the woman, or the Light, if there is anything else you need to know right now."

I calmed myself down and focused on the image of the woman.

"You need to get going," I said.

Anne started to laugh. "I need to get going?"

"That's what she said."

"Tell her I'm working on it, and, when you're ready, bring your awareness back to the room."

I could feel the look of disgust on my face as the feeling of despair flooded my chest like heavy, dark molasses. All I could focus on was the thought that there were others.

"I have no recollection of there being anyone but my father."

"Maybe you shouldn't take it literally."

I knew it was true, but I had enough on my plate. Anne would be gone soon and I was afraid to open any more wounds.

"Did the message about the book mean anything to you?"

"No. I don't know what I'd write a book about."

"I imagine it would be about what you're experiencing."

"I'm not writing about this. I can barely stand living it."

"Are you interested in writing at all?"

I told her I had a passion to write as a child, but my spelling was so bad, I didn't think I had the talent.

"If it was a childhood interest, you most likely have some natural writing talent. It might also help you move through some of these feelings if you return to your passion."

I appreciated her encouragement, but I wasn't in the mood. The days ahead were looking darker. I had been through so much, yet it felt as though the process had only just begun.

"Writing is not what I need right now," I said.

She looked at me like she could read my mind. Like she felt my pain. "Would it be alright if I just held you?"

I nodded. "I always want you to hold me."

She sat down on the couch next to me and put her arms around me. I leaned my head on her shoulders and rested my hand on her bare arm. The connection between us was so strong and so loving.

"Knowing you were here made this bearable," I said.

"Yes, I know what you mean."

I closed my eyes. The moment felt so good, so warm, but all I could think of was how quickly it would be gone. Our relationship was limited by time, by boundaries. And no matter how much I needed her, that wasn't enough to keep her from leaving.

"Do you really have to go?" I asked.

"I think we both know the answer to that. If I stay here any longer, I'm afraid I'll just be getting in your way."

Sadly, she was right. I found the comfort I had longed for in her. And ironically it was keeping me from fully feeling the pain of not having it when I needed it as a child.

"You're not going to forget about me, are you?"

"I'm never going to forget you. You are very much a part of me."

She got up and took a picture out of her purse. "Here, I want you to have this."

The photo was a close-up of her in a denim dress holding a small white rabbit. Her smile filled her slender cheeks. The rabbit seemed at peace in her arms.

"Sometimes," she said, "when we get away from relationships that are as intense and connected as ours, we question whether they really happened at all. I just want you to know I was here, and this was real." She sat down again and put her arms back around me. I couldn't find the words to describe how much she meant to me, so I closed my eyes and traveled past my thoughts, escaping in her arms to a place deep inside myself.

"I love you very much," I said.

"I love you, too."

She held me tighter and suddenly the inside of my body felt numb. I opened my eyes and looked at my hand. It was resting against her arm, but it didn't feel like it was attached to my body. I moved my fingers to feel her skin. The emotional breaker switch in my mind had gone off, and the sensation of touch was gone.

"I wish I could wrap you up and take you with me," she said. "Hold you in my arms where I know you'd be safe. But as much as I love you, I can't protect you from your past."

My past. I was trying so hard to stay connected to her, but I could not control my mind from disconnecting from my body. I crossed my hands as she held me, then slowly dug my fingernail into my palm. I could no longer feel my skin. When I spoke, my voice sounded like it was coming from the other side of the room.

"Anne, I have to go. But before I do, I just want to tell you that someday I hope you see yourself the way I see you."

"How's that?"

"There is something very special about you, and it doesn't seem like you know it."

She smiled. "I have a feeling that's the point of my trip. I'm going into phase two."

"There are two phases to this journey?"

"For me there are. But, knowing you, you'll probably do it all at once."

She got up and handed me a note while I picked up my keys and stood by the door, frozen out of the moment.

"I'm going to miss you very much," she said as we embraced.

I felt enclosed in a jar--my hands pressed against the glass, desperate to feel the warmth of her body, suffocating from the lack of oxygen.

I kept my eyes on the floor and walked out the door. When I reached my car, I opened her note.

I believe that the thoughts of those who love you can make a difference. That's why I want you to know I'm thinking of you now.

I know for a time we will not be able to see or speak to each other. First, that will be <u>temporary</u>. But secondly, I want you to know that I carry you, very alive, in my heart. And you can always reach me by doing the same. Now is the time to call upon faith and use it. Because what we have had, and do have, is very real and no one can take that from you, ever! I believe in <u>you</u>. You're going to be fine, I know it!

Love,
Anne

I put the note and the picture in my purse then rested my head against the window. I still couldn't feel my body. I stared up at the sky. My mind blank until a voice in my head told me to go home.

The next day, I awoke feeling as if a loved one had died; you forget at first, then it all comes flooding back. Jeff had taken Matthew and Jen to their schools and Isabella took Katie to meet up with one of her friends in the neighborhood. The house was quiet. I called Laura and got her voice mail. Then I called Cynthia, the neighbor who was also a client of Anne's. I asked her to coffee and an hour later we met at the harbor.

Cynthia walked up with her youngest in a stroller. I picked up our drinks and we sat down at an outside table. Cynthia started talking from the moment she saw me and had barely taken a breath since. There was drama going on at the elementary school between two of the teachers and that seemed to segue into some neighborhood gossip. I started to partially listen until she said, "I saw Anne last week."

I felt a jolt inside my body.

"You know she's leaving on Monday to Asia."

"Yes. I saw her yesterday. I guess her plans suddenly changed."

She looked slightly perturbed.

"She's been planning to go to Thailand since last spring. She might not have told you. Anne thought clients would stop coming to see her if they knew. She has a thing about that."

"What?"

A shock of panic ran up my spine exploding in my head. Everything in my body started to tingle and the ground felt like it was starting to spin.

I jumped up from the table and grabbed my keys.

"What's wrong?" Cynthia asked as she leaned back.

"Everything."

I raced home, ran upstairs to the loft, and called Anne's office.

"I'm sorry, the number you have reached is no longer in service."

I slammed down the phone and threw a book against the wall. "Damn it! How did I let this happen!" I rifled through my desk, found Anne's number and called her at home. On the second ring she answered.

"Did you lie to me?" I yelled.

"What?"

"Did you lie to me? Had you been planning to leave the entire time and you didn't tell me because you thought I'd quit therapy."

"Dawn, you're going to have to back up. Where's this coming from?"

The calm tone of her voice started to bring me back to my senses. I leaned my back against the wall and slowly slid to the floor. I knew better than this. Anne wouldn't have lied to me.

"I'm so sorry... I just saw Cynthia. She said you have known you were leaving for a long time and you didn't tell me because I was a client."

"I don't know what Cynthia thinks she knows, but I assure you I told you right after I made the decision."

I was stuck. I felt embarrassed about my actions, frustrated by feelings I couldn't quite name.

"I'm sorry," I said. "There's something very strange happening to me. I didn't mean to call you at home. I'm sorry."

"It's okay, Dawn. I know this is upsetting to you."

"No, it's not okay. I'm sorry. I really have to go now," I said as I hung up.

I tried to stand up and my knees began to buckle. I grabbed my phone book off the nightstand and laid on the floor. It took forever to find Judith's number, then three tries to dial it correctly. When she answered, I tried to tell her what had happened, but I wasn't making much sense.

"Where are you?" she asked.

"I'm at home. I need some help."

"I have some free time this afternoon. Why don't you meet me at my office?"

"I can't move, Judith. I can't even see straight."

"What's your address? I'm coming over."

Twenty minutes later she walked upstairs to find me lying on the floor. She put down her purse and sat next to me.

"What's this all about?"

I tried again to explain what I'd heard from Cynthia and my phone call to Anne.

"What were you doing going to coffee with one of Anne's clients?"

"She's also a neighbor."

"Dawn, you set up that coffee because she knows Anne."

My shoulders sank lower than the carpet. "How could I have been so stupid? How could I have let somebody in my heart like this? I feel like such an idiot."

"This is not your fault."

"Yes, it is. I should not have listened to Cynthia. I shouldn't have called Anne, and I shouldn't have..." I lost track of my thoughts.

"Dawn, you are being re-abused, and that is not your fault." I turned away and stared at the wall. "Where are the kids?"

"They're at school."

"Good. I wasn't sure how you were going to handle Anne's leaving, but to play it safe, I'd like to put you in the hospital."

"Hospital? I'm not psychotic. I'm just having a bad day."

"No, this is more than a bad day. It's a breakdown."

I clenched my jaw and stared back at her. "No, it's not!"

"Dawn, I've kept my mouth shut while you went back to see Anne, but that's over now. She's leaving the country in a few days, and when she does, you're going to have to realize that there is no rescue."

"What are you talking about?"

"There's no relationship on the face of this earth that will ever rescue you or compensate for the pain you suffered as a child."

"I didn't expect Anne to rescue me."

"I'm sure you didn't, but there's a five-year old rape victim that lives inside of you and she's been hanging on to Anne for dear life."

Her words hit hard. If I had sunk any further, I would have been in the room below.

"That child is still stuck in the closet waiting for some-body to come and make the pain go away. And it's not going to happen. Our adult relationships cannot compensate for what we didn't get as children."

"But the need for her is so strong."

"Because it's an old need, a childhood need. You have to allow yourself to feel the pain of that need not being filled, and you do that by being true to yourself--and honest about your relationship with Anne."

"I was honest."

"Dawn, you've been using the facade of therapy to go back and see her all summer."

"Being a client was the only way I could see her."

"So, instead of suffering the pain of losing Anne, you became something you weren't in order to get something you needed."

"It's more complicated than that."

"When we change ourselves to fit somebody else's ideals or parameters, we are not being true to who we are in the world."

"Anne wasn't going to change her parameters for me."

"Then have the strength to walk away."

Tearing out the inside of my body would have been less painful. "I don't know if I can do that."

"You don't have a choice anymore."

Big round tears began to roll down my face. The release felt like the first drops off an iceberg.

"Dawn, its time you acknowledge your losses and feel your pain."

"That could last forever."

"Not if you really feel it. And if you do, then eventually the pain will go, and you will learn to see life in a different way."

I pulled my knees to my chest. "This hurts so badly."

"It's supposed to hurt. You have had more losses this year than most people could tolerate. It's going to take some time to work through them, and the hospital has a good program to help you do that."

"I'm not going into the hospital."

"I'm going to recommend the out-patient program. You can come home at night."

I tried to get up, but the dizziness sent me back down.

"What do you do there?"

"You'll spend the day in small therapy groups."

"I don't want to talk to other people."

"Everybody says that, but you'll be better off in a group than you will be sitting here in your room curled up on the floor."

"Will I still see you?"

"Don't worry, I'm not letting you out of my sight."

Jeff walked into the bedroom just as Judith was leaving. She filled him in on the plan then he walked Judith out to her car. Shortly after, he came upstairs with a plate of scrambled eggs and toast. I'm not sure what Judith had told him, but he was much kinder than he had been in some time. He sat down next to me and rested his hand on my leg.

"You're really brave to do this," he said.

"I'm sorry, Jeff. I'm so sorry that this is all happening." I started to cry.

"This isn't your fault."

"Yeah, I keep hearing that, but I feel like I'm letting down you and the kids."

"You are not letting us down."

I shook my head. "Judith says I only have to stay until 5pm each day. I'll take care of the kids as soon as I get home and I will be there for them until I have to leave in the morning."

"Don't worry about that. Isabella and I can take care of the kids. Just focus on getting better."

I dropped my head onto his shoulder.

"I'm going to call your parents and tell them what's happening to you. Maybe this will get their attention."

I shook my head. "I'm sure it will just send them further away."

"If that's their response, then we don't need them in our lives."

I nodded. Jeff's mother had moved away, and my mom was the only grandparent the kids had a relationship with. I didn't want that loss for the kids, or for my mother.

"We can talk about that later," I said as I took a bite of toast then put the meal to the side.

He kissed me on the forehead. "We don't have to talk about it at all if you don't want."

Isabella walked in a few minutes after Jeff left the bedroom.

"Dawn, you no bueno?"

"No Isabella, me no bueno."

"Ok. You get better. Me muy bueno con la bebes. No worry. Me play, play, play con Jen y Matthew y Katie. Si. No worry. Bebes ok con me."

"Gracias Isabella. Gracias. I'm so sorry."

"No necesario sorry. It's ok, Dawn, it's ok."

CHAPTER EIGHT

On Monday morning, Anne Myers boarded a plane to Thailand, and I surrendered myself into a six-week outpatient program at the local psychiatric hospital. I put on my jeans, a black turtleneck, and my ankle-high boots. It was my best don't-mess-with-me outfit, and it gave me some sense of protection--otherwise I felt like hell.

The hospital was a few miles from my house. I drove up early and walked around the spacious grounds, a series of one-story stucco buildings sprawled through an old eucalyptus grove that covered the area in leaves. The trees towered over the compound. Fields of long-stemmed wildflowers separated the buildings.

I walked down a path to the center courtyard, a grassy bluff with a gazebo that overlooked the harbor. I stood for a moment and watched a sailboat leave the jetty. The view was in black and white--a picture I couldn't taste, touch or feel. The world it seemed had lost all its color.

Judith had arranged for me to meet with Dr. Bryant, a slender black-Asian man with short hair and a neatly trimmed beard who wore a gray fitted crew neck sweater that accentuated his lean body. We met in the lobby of the main building where a line of young girls stood against the wall outside of the cafeteria. We said hello and he led me across the campus.

"What's with the girls against the wall?"

"This side of the campus is where the teens are admitted for treatment. The girls you saw are being treated for eating disorders. They have to remain supervised in the lobby for 30 minutes after they eat."

"Who else is here?"

"Adults and teens dealing with depression or suicide. We also have some teen gang members that have opted for psychological treatment instead of incarceration." He stopped in front of a door and looked at me. "It's a treatment center. It's not *One Flew Over the Cuckoo's Nest*."

He opened the door and led me into a small, sterile conference room with a wooden table and two metal chairs. I kept my hands in my jeans and pulled my chair out with my boot.

"How are you feeling this morning?" he asked.

"I'm fine."

"I talked to Judith this weekend. She said you and Anne were very close."

"My being here has nothing to do with Anne."

"I know Anne. She's a good therapist."

"I'm not here to talk about my therapist. I'm here to recover from child abuse."

He looked at me while he rubbed his short black beard. "Dawn, if you cared for Anne and you trusted her to care for you, then I imagine that having her leave the country in the middle of your therapy is very difficult."

"It was, but it's not now. I've accepted that she had to leave and now I'm getting on with my life."

"Just like that?"

"Yes, just like that." I got out of my chair and leaned against the wall.

"Do you see any similarities between the abandonment you felt from your parents and Anne leaving your therapeutic relationship?"

I kicked the chair up against the table and began to raise my voice. "Look, my dad was sick and mistreated me. My mother was too naive to know any better. And Anne had a life to lead. I was just a client."

He nodded. "That's interesting. Who's protecting you?"

"What do you mean?"

"While you're protecting your father, your mother, and Anne, who's protecting you?"

"The only person who can... me."

"Then why don't you start by realizing that whether it was intentional or not, all of these people have hurt you, and if you ever want to get out of this depression, you're going to have to stop rationalizing away their actions and start to feel some of the pain it's causing you. I think the best place to start is with your relationship with Anne."

"She's gone!" I yelled. "I don't care about her anymore. Let's just get on with the child abuse issues." I kicked my chair, tears flooding down my cheeks.

"Why are you crying?"

"You frustrate me! Is this session over yet?"

"In a minute. Judith wanted me to review you for an antidepressant. I have decided not to put you on one."

"Why?"

"Medication is not a cure. It only treats symptoms, and you don't strike me as somebody who is interested in managing symptoms."

"I just want to be well so I can get back to my children."

"It may be more difficult, but I think an antidepressant would just slow you down."

"Fine, I didn't want to take one anyway."

He stood up. "I'll give you a few minutes alone, and then I want to introduce you to the group."

He left and I started to cry. It felt like tears that I had been holding back my entire life were racing to the surface to be released. I don't know how long I had been sitting in the corner sobbing when he reentered the room.

"Come on," he said, "let's go for a walk."

He circled me around a path through the grounds until my tears had stopped then we entered another building and into a therapy group to meet the other patients. The room was small, with straw colored grass-cloth walls and no windows. Four chairs and a couch were grouped around an old, narrow-legged coffee table, set on a white-speckled linoleum floor that reminded me of my childhood bathroom. I sat on the couch next to a woman wearing a long-sleeved white shirt and a pair of jeans, her jaw muscle clenched so tight it extended beyond her ears. I said hello. She stared at a wall and jiggled her foot up and down on the floor.

The three women across from me were more congenial. We smiled at each other as Dr. Bryant began the group discussion.

"We have a new member today." Dr. Bryant introduced me and then asked the group to share what they wanted about why they were there.

Liz, a petite well-dressed woman with short, graying hair and a pale, brazen face, spoke first. She was a senior vice president for IBM. "I had a nervous breakdown on a flight to New York," she said. "Other than that, I grew up in a slum in Texas, got married to put myself through college, and became suicidal after my last promotion."

"Why was that?" I asked.

She turned over the palms of her hands to show me several deep disfiguring scars that looked like potholes burnt into red flash. "This is where my mother used to put out her cigarettes," she said. "I've been working my whole life just to prove I was worth more than an ashtray."

The woman next to her was Maria, a short, round, middle-aged Hispanic woman who worked at the local post office. Tears wrapped in black mascara rolled down her checks as she spoke about a recent shooting at the office that killed six of her coworkers. She could barely speak as she shared that two bullets hit the man in front of her sparing her own life. "It's been six months, and this is the first time I've been out of my house."

Next to me on the couch was Patty with the tight jaw, a boyish looking woman in her late twenties with flaky, white skin and thin long brown hair. She said hello in a low voice, but she didn't look at me and she didn't say why she was there. Oddly, I felt most comfortable sitting next to her. She felt familiar. Almost like a sister.

Dr. Bryant began by reading a meditation out of a small book. The book was passed around the room and each member commented on what the meditation meant to her. I wasn't sure if it was rigged or a coincidence, but the meditation of the day was entitled *Loss*.

When the book made its way to Patty her bouncing foot accelerated.

"Pass," she said as she handed me the book.

"You can do that?" I asked Dr. Bryant.

"Maybe she doesn't have anything to share."

I looked at the book. "Loss. I don't think I have anything to share either."

Dr. Bryant looked at me. "Your therapist left the country today on a sabbatical. Would you like to share with the group your feelings around her leaving?"

I felt the eyes of the other members on me, as my stomach cramped with a yearning to be held by Anne.

"Yes, she did." I stared at the table. "But there really isn't anything to talk about. I just came to trust, and, I guess, to love her very deeply. It was a special relationship."

Liz started to laugh, and I felt myself start to shrink. "Dawn, everybody falls in love with their therapist. It's the oldest one in the book."

"It is?"

"Yes. They are like objects we mold to fit our needs. We create them by imagining they are everything we ever needed in a person. It happens all the time."

I shook my head. "No, it wasn't like that. I know she cared for me just as much."

"You think your therapist loved you?" Liz asked.

"Yes, I do."

"Dawn, what makes you think that?" Dr. Bryant asked.

"She told me." I regretted the words as soon as they left my mouth.

"Your therapist told you she loved you," Liz said as she raised her eyebrows.

"It sounds like some emotional boundaries were crossed," Dr. Bryant said. "Does your new therapist know about this?"

"These damned therapists are always abusing their power. You ought to report her for that," Maria said.

Report her? Why would I want to report her?

"That's all I have to say." I handed the book to Dr. Bryant and sank into the couch.

Everybody falls in love with their therapist. Great. I wasn't just an idiot, I was a common idiot.

The morning session was followed by lunch, an anger management class, another group process meeting, and then closing comments. At five o'clock we went home. At nine o'clock each morning, we met in the same small room.

By the end of the week, we were starting to bond. Liz and I were probably the closest, our contempt for authority figures the common bond. Patty was the only group member who hadn't participated. Each day she sat next to me, her leg crossed in my direction, her foot shaking like a rattling engine. By the end of the week, the vibration on the couch was driving me crazy. Out of sheer irritation, I found the nerve to grab her tennis shoe.

"Why are you here?" I asked as I stared at her.

She looked at me for the first time. "I'm a cutter."

"What's a cutter?"

She pulled up her sleeve and showed me the deep, red grooves that lined her arm.

"Sometimes I can't feel my body. The only way I can tell if I'm still alive is to cut my arm until I feel pain." She pushed down her sleeves. "I'm also a lesbian and a bulimic, if that helps you any."

"You mean you actually make yourself throw up?"

"No, I can do it by will. Want to see?"

"No thanks." There was a brief pause before the more compelling question jumped out of my mouth. "So how do you know you're a lesbian?"

She smirked. "Because the idea of putting some guy's dick inside of me makes me want to vomit."

"Is that how you throw up at will?"

She smiled and befriended me with a nod. "Believe me, being a lesbian isn't a sexuality anybody wants to sign up for."

"Why not?"

"Are you kidding? You're ostracized from society, it's not easy to have children, and imagine how difficult it would be to be in love with a woman who has as many emotional needs as you do. You guys with husbands have it easy. All you have to do is hand them a beer and turn on a football game."

She got up and poured herself some coffee.

"Do you ever wish you were straight?" Liz asked in her IBM executive tone.

"Hell, no! Men are simple, but they're still hairy, disgusting pigs."

Liz and I looked at each other and smiled. "I think my husband's a pig. Does that mean I'm a lesbian?" Liz said.

"Yeah, and I fell in love with my therapist, does that mean I'm a lesbian?"

Patty stirred her coffee, opened the door, and looked at us. "You guys aren't gay. You're just fucked up."

Liz and I looked at each other and laughed.

"She should be a therapist."

"I'd go to her," I said.

"So would I. That was the best diagnosis I've ever received."

When I came home that evening, Jeff was sitting bare chested in front of the television with a cold beer in his hand watching a football game. Three empty cans were stacked in a pyramid on the coffee table. He grabbed me by the waist and pulled me into his lap.

"It's fourth down, the 49ers are on the fifty-yard line. They're losing by six points. This play could be crucial!"

I put my arm around him. "Where are the kids?"

"They're upstairs watching a movie with Isabella."

I stayed on his lap until the play was over then gave him a kiss and walked up stairs, thinking about Patty's comments, appreciating how simple Jeff really was.

The kids were in the playroom, their hair still wet from a bath, wearing Jeff's freshly laundered T-shirts he always put them in after he pulled them out of the tub.

"Mom! Mom! Mom!" they yelled as they all ran over and jumped on me.

"Where have you been all day?"

"Mommy in es school," said Isabella as we changed places on the couch. I pulled Katie onto my lap while Jen and Matthew snuggled around me, grounding me back to earth like landing after a turbulent flight.

"That's right," I smiled at Isabella as she left the room. "I go to a school that is helping me understand some things about life, and it's helping me to feel better so that sometime soon I'll be able to spend more time with you."

"What do you learn?" Jen asked.

"I learn things like… sometimes people don't treat us very nicely because they don't feel very good about themselves."

"Like when people are mean to you?"

"Yes. Sometimes people are mean or hurtful because they don't really understand how much it hurts us when they are."

She nodded her head like she knew exactly what I was talking about.

"Mommy," Matthew said, "how much longer do you have to go to school?"

"A few more weeks, Honey. Just a few more weeks."

I pushed through my exhaustion to listen to their stories about the day: the chocolate popsicle that Matthew was given at a school party, the substitute teacher that asked Jen to read a story to the class, and the new nursery rhyme Katie acted out with her fingers. I looked at the little pink palms of her hands as she sang--and thought about Liz. How could a mother put out a cigarette on such innocent flesh, and cause such soul crushing harm?

When the kids began to settle down, I tucked them each into bed and went into my room. The football game was over, and Jeff was in bed with his hands resting behind his head, and his legs opened as he sprawled out between the covers. He looked at me with a boyish grin, his eyelids slightly drooping, as if the adrenaline from the game was wearing off, and the beer was setting in.

"Come to bed," he said in a low inviting voice.

"Be there in a minute," I replied as I walked into the bathroom and closed the door. I knew if I took long enough to brush my teeth and wash my face, he'd be asleep when I returned, and I could avoid the guilt of rejecting him. A few minutes later, I heard a light snore from the bedroom. I quietly opened the door and crawled into bed. When I closed my eyes, the image of the woman in the shawl appeared, and in the background was the Light. Each time it appeared it looked a little larger and I couldn't tell if I was coming closer to it, or it was coming closer to me.

New members had arrived in the hospital program that week including a prostitute, an 18-year-old pyromaniac, and a TV producer who had just attempted suicide. Our group had become an intriguing mix of successful businesswomen and petty felons. Yet despite our social differences, it didn't take long for all of us to bond. As we shared our stories and bared our souls, it became clear that we all had the same wound. At our core we felt like we were defective and worthless. Undeserving of love. Our only difference was our motives. Half of the women in our group were trying to prove they were worthy. While the other half, were trying to prove that they weren't.

Friday's morning meditation was on abandonment. I tensed when I heard the word. I had been in such emotional pain since Anne left that I found it difficult to breathe, but I wasn't sure if it was because I felt abandoned by her, or temporarily set aside.

Liz handed me the book. "I pass." They all looked at me. I hadn't said anything about Anne in group since my first day in the program and Liz looked as if she was ready to call me out. I stared back at her.

"I said, I pass."

She let it go.

The afternoon group met on the lawn. Liz, Patty and I grabbed a cup of coffee and stayed behind on the couch.

"What is the deal with your therapist?" Liz asked. "You look like you've been jilted by a lover."

I tried to explain the relationship, but the love I felt for Anne didn't seem to translate.

"Was it sexual?" Liz asked.

"No. I wasn't physically attracted to her. But my love for her was so strong it sure makes me question my sexuality." I looked at Patty. "Are you sure I'm not gay?"

"Are you sexually attracted to women?"

"Not really. But to tell the truth, I'm so hungry to be nurtured I'd have sex with a woman just to be held."

Patty hit me across the knee. "Don't do that."

"Why not?"

"First of all, you don't want to mislead a well-intentioned lesbian just because you want to be held. And, secondly, being nurtured should not cost you anything. Sex for affection is what your father taught you, and there are other ways to find the comfort you need."

"Patty, I'm a grown woman. What am I supposed to do? Walk up to somebody and say, 'Excuse me, I have the emotional mentality of a five-year-old, could you please hold me?'"

"It's better than saying, 'If you hold me, I'll give you sex.'" She shook her head. "At some point in your life, you're going to have to have more respect for your body than that."

I reached down and lifted her self-defiled arm.

"Really?"

She grinned. "Funny how we tell each other what we need to hear."

Liz put down her coffee. "I don't understand," she said. "Did this therapist fall in love with you?"

"I don't know exactly how she feels about me. I only know that she loves me."

"Is she married?" Patty asked.

"Yes, but she didn't leave with her husband."

They looked at each other and started to laugh. "Dawn, somebody wouldn't have to be gay to be attracted to you," Liz said.

"If she was attracted to me, she hid it well. I never sensed it was sexual. It felt more like she had taken me as her child."

"That's not healthy either," Liz said.

"Maybe not. But I needed it. It felt like she was my first maternal bond, and it sparked something in me."

"Like what?" Liz asked.

"My soul."

"Sounds like she's running from you," Patty said.

Running from me? I wanted to believe it, but it didn't feel true.

"No, she's not running from me. She's out looking for herself."

I saw Dr. Bryant that afternoon. We met privately twice a week for a brief check-in. Each appointment with him seemed to be more frustrating than the last. I respected him, but I didn't want to trust him, and I didn't want to care about him. The conflict I felt in our sessions, made my skin crawl and the frustration drove me to tears. While my reactions intrigued him, I was just glad our meetings were brief.

When I pulled up to the house that evening the kid's bikes were in the yard and there were sticks of broken chalk on the sidewalk where they colored on the cement. The garage door was half opened and Jeff was hitting the punching bag with a rage so fierce I could feel it from the street. I got out of the car and quietly walked in the front door. Isabella met me in the entry way to tell me that Matthew and Katie had been fighting all day and Jen had been in her room since she came home from school.

"Que pasa, Isabella?"

"No sé. The bebés no happy today. You no happy, Jeff no happy, me no happy."

"I'm sorry. I know it's mucho trabajo for you. I'm trying to be happy again. Muy rapido."

"No Dawn. Me understand. Your padre no bueno. I know. I know. Mi padre no bueno, too. All day me cry, cry, cry. Como you. Me too, Dawn, me too."

Tears filled in both our eyes as we stared at each other in the dim entry way. We came from different worlds. We had different means. Yet beyond everything that was different about us, we too shared the same unseeable wound. A wound that I was coming to know more as the norm, than the exception.

"Usted necesitas help?" I asked.

"No, mi madre es muy strong. She cuida de mi. I'm okay now. I'm okay," she said.

Her mother took care of her. What a difference that would have made.

That night Jen woke up with leg cramps. Her cries tugged me from a heavy sleep, so deep and timeless I thought I was a child, and the cries were coming from me.

"I'll get her," Jeff said sarcastically. His back turned to me, with no intention of moving. The energy around his body felt hostile and it was becoming clearer that he was waging a silent strike against picking up anything around the house.

"Mom," she cried out again. "I need you." I jumped out of bed and ran to her room. When I got to her bedside, her leg was tucked to her chest, and she was holding on to her small gangly calf. I pulled her legs across my lap and started massaging the muscle.

"It's okay, Baby. You're just having some growing pains."

I grabbed a heating pad from the drawer, wrapped it around her leg, and got into bed next to her. She wrapped her arms around my waist and rested her head on my stomach.

"Will you stay with me tonight?"

"Yes Baby, I'll stay right here." I kissed the top of her head and leaned my shoulders against the wall as she tucked her head into my chest.

"Mommy?"

"Yes."

"Dad says Grampa is a bad man."

I let out a deep sigh. "Yes. He has done some very bad things."

"Do we ever have to see him again?"

"No, we never have to see him again."

"Good, he makes me feel weird."

My heart started to race, and I could feel my face flush. "Did he ever hurt you in any way?" I asked.

"No. I just don't like the way he hugs."

I held her tighter. "Well, I promise you that will never happen again."

I kissed her on the head and we both dosed off to sleep. At 3:00 a.m., I was awakened by a full moon framed in the bedroom window. When I closed my eyes, I saw the face of Dr. Bryant as a thought pushed through my mind.

He will help you.

The following day, I was sitting in a group session about the benefits of good nutrition. The material was familiar to me so I rested my head in my hand and dozed off. Suddenly, a photo of a naked child appeared in my mind, and I was overwhelmed with a wave of nausea. Afraid I was going to be ill, I stood up and went outside to get some fresh air. My knees trembled as I walked to the lawn while my mind flashed abstract images of a naked girl lying flat on a beige-carpeted floor. The fear that I was about to be killed poured through every cell in my body, like I was defenseless in a dark alley and about to be ambushed.

My heart began to pound through my ears and my mouth felt like a desert. I crossed the lawn and walked toward the cafeteria for a drink. It was an hour before lunch and the only two people in the commons were a nurse and Dr. Bryant. I went up and told him what was happening. He looked down at my trembling hands.

"My appointment just canceled," he said. "Let's see if we can find a room to talk."

He walked me into a small conference room. I sat down on the couch while he took the chair.

"What's going on?"

"It feels like a memory and it's making me sick."

"You are okay. Just take a few breaths." He pulled a pen out of his bag and leaned back in his chair. "How are you most comfortable retrieving your memories?"

"Anne would have me close my eyes and focus on the feeling. Then images usually appear."

"Is that what you want to do?"

"I guess."

"Okay, then close your eyes and focus on what you are experiencing."

I took a few more deep breaths and closed my eyes. When I did, all I could see in my mind was thick gray fog.

"It's very foggy," I said.

"What else do you notice?"

"It's early in the morning. I can barely see where I am." I felt the cold dampness of the early morning fog that often rolled in along the coast in the beach town where I grew up. "I'm in the car with my dad. We're at a park."

"How old are you?"

"I'm six. There are two men in the fog... no, they're in the window. They're watching me with my dad."

"Do you know the men?"

"Yes, Mr. Thomas and Mr. Unger; they're my dad's friends. I'm afraid they're going to come in. My dad tells me I'm safe... he's protecting me."

My voice started to crack. "I feel my dad's protection. I feel the strength of his body... but... but he's the one who brought me here." Tears streamed down my cheeks. *'Don't leave, Dad. Please don't leave.'*

"What's happening, Dawn?"

My eyes opened and I stared at the floor. "He said he was going to walk down the hill to have a cigarette. When he got out of the car, Mr. Unger got in." I felt my stomach tighten. "My pants were off and he started to touch me," I said as a wave of shame melted me into a puddle of filth.

"What happened next? How do you respond?"

"I do nothing. I just hold my breath and wait for it to be over."

The picture took center stage in my mind, like it had been pressed into my brain with a branding iron.

"When Mr. Unger was through with me, he showed me a picture. A Polaroid picture of a dead girl lying on a beige carpet. He said he was my friend and he wanted to protect me. He told me bad things happen when little girls talk, and he didn't want to see anything bad happen to me." The picture of the naked child was as clear as the day I first saw it. She appeared to be about ten-years-old, her skin fair and her body long and skinny like mine. Long, brownish-blonde hair fell limp around her soft round face. Her eyes were closed, and her small, bluish lips curved down toward a red blood-stained slit that ran around the center of her neck.

I rested my head in my hands. "I knew I was never supposed to remember this. These men are going to kill me. They're going to kill me!" I felt as if my life was over. I pulled my knees to my chest and curled up into a ball.

"No, they're not," Dr. Bryant said. "They can't hurt that little girl anymore. You grew up, and you're safe."

"No, I'm not! I'm not safe anywhere!"

He handed me some tissue as I lifted my head and took some deep breaths.

"How could he share me with his friends?" I cried. "How could he give me away like that?"

"I'm sorry."

I felt like a naked child in front of three grown men, the shame covering me like indelible ink.

"Is this real? Did this really happen to me?"

"It looks real to me. I'm not sure if the fog you describe was part of the memory, or if your mind wasn't ready to see it clearly. But I believe it happened."

"How? How could I forget this?"

"If children can't remove themselves from danger, their minds do it for them."

My head began to hurt, more from the confusion than the memory.

"But I loved my dad. Honestly, he meant everything to me. Wouldn't I have hated him for doing this?"

"We need our parents' love to survive. That's why kids blame themselves for abuse."

I picked up a pillow from the couch and held it against my chest. "Could anything else be causing this? A brain tumor, a nightmare, anything?"

"I'm sorry, Dawn. There is no other phenomena to explain what you've been experiencing."

I stared at him, shaking my head in disbelief.

"Dawn, I can't tell you what all happened to you as a child, but in order to heal from this ordeal you're going to have to trust your feelings."

"How can I trust my feelings when I've been betrayed by my own memory?"

"Your memory didn't betray you. It protected you."

I wanted to die. When it was just my father, I could hold on to the belief that I was special. That in his own demented way he loved me. But this memory shattered everything I had left. The degradation felt so deep I didn't ever want to be seen again by another human being.

Dr. Bryant stayed with me for the next hour and then walked me back to my group. On the path back, I noticed my body and the gait of my walk. Although I had always been athletic, I had never been able to touch my toes. Even in grade school, I could only bend to my knees. But suddenly I felt different. More limber. I reached down and touched my toes. It was as if I carried that memory like a metal bar that had finally been released from my lower spine.

"Wow," I said to Dr. Bryant. "We really do store memories in our body."

"Memories like that, we have to put somewhere. You would not have been able to function as a child if you didn't lock it away."

I looked at him, feeling how calm I now felt in his presence.

"Thank you," I said. "I feel at peace with you."

"I'm sorry you had to go through that."

"Me too."

I came home that night and called my sister. She was 4 years younger than me and we had never been close. But, when I told her about the abuse, although it had not happened to her, she believed me. She knew I would not have made something so horrible up, and she also knew how much I loved our dad. When I told her about the latest memory, she recalled both the men. Mr. Thomas had been an architect who worked with my dad. Mr. Unger was a pharmacist, and a skin-diving buddy who would often stop by the house. She then told me that Mr. Unger had been in jail for over a decade. He had been convicted for running the largest steroid ring in Southern California. It was a sick kind of validation, the kind that made me want to hang up and crawl into bed.

In the morning I woke up enraged, and before Jeff and the kids got up, I ran to the beach to try and calm myself down. After four miles, I still had the desire to kill. I came back to the garage, grabbed a baseball bat and started swinging it as hard as I could into the heavy bag. When the bat broke, I threw it into the garage door and went inside to call Judith.

"I'm not going to the hospital today," I said.

"What's going on?"

I told her about the new memories, and she asked me to come into her office. An hour later, I blasted through her door.

"Where the fuck is Anne?" I yelled.

She looked up from her chair. "Why is that important to you right now?"

"Because I need her!" I grabbed a pillow and threw it onto the couch. "I have to tell her about the memories. Damn it! Why isn't she here?"

The pain tore through the anger, and I doubled over in tears.

"I need her. I need her to hold me."

Judith got up and sat next to me on the couch. "Dawn, don't you think this is what you felt like when you were a child? You had just been molested by your father and his friends, and you wanted to have a mother you could come home to--a mother who would understand your pain and hold you in her arms."

"But I don't want my mom to hold me. I want Anne to."

I stood up and walked across the room.

"I know you want Anne right now. But the intensity of the emotions you're dealing with isn't just about Anne. It's about all the experiences in your life that have been similar and never expressed. It's called transference phenomenon."

"Transference phenomenon? There's a name for this?"

"Yes. It's rare for a patient to feel the misery of their childhood by way of direct memories. Their memories are either banished or dissociated from any kind of feelings. But the real history of the person often shows in the feelings and behavior toward a current reference person, like a therapist."

"So my feelings about Anne are really about my parents?"

"I think that many of them are."

I shook my head. "I've been in therapy for a year. Why am I just now hearing about this?"

"I've been trying to get you to look at the similar feelings you have for Anne and your parents for months."

"Yes, but you never told me why."

"It's the therapist's responsibility to pick up on the transferences, not the clients."

"That's ridiculous. Anne could not read my mind. And neither can you."

"You're right, but would it have made a difference if you had known?"

"Yes. It would have helped me understand why my feelings for her have been killing me."

"Dawn, up to the time Anne left you hadn't been showing any emotion."

"That doesn't mean I haven't been having any." I turned around and hit the wall with the palm of my hand. "I hate this relationship."

"Our relationship?"

"The therapeutic relationship."

"Why do you hate it?"

"It's unfair, unbalanced, and it threatens my dignity!"

"Like being molested by adults?"

"If that's a transference, then yes. Therapy to me is like being molested by adults. You have the power and I get screwed."

Judith handed me a tissue and sat back in her chair. I walked over to the couch and slid down in my seat. "What a waste of time," I said.

"What's been a waste of time?"

"Therapy. I was very careful about the feelings I shared with Anne. I was ashamed of how needy and neurotic I was feeling so I kept those thoughts to myself. If I had known those feelings had more to do with my childhood than they did with Anne, I would have been free to explore them."

"Anne's a therapist. She would have seen your feelings as transferences, not as needy or neurotic."

"Yes, but I didn't know that, and I didn't know she knew that."

"But she was your therapist. You were supposed to be talking to her about your thoughts and feelings."

I shook my head. "You don't understand. I needed Anne. I needed her to love and care about me. I wanted her to like me as a person, not see me as some whining, irrational pain-in-the-ass."

"What was the fear of showing her all your feelings?"

"That she'd leave. That she wouldn't want to see me again."

"She did leave."

Tears rolled down my face. "Yes, but that wasn't because of me."

"That's right. We cannot control other people's actions by our behavior. You could have proved to Anne that you were the best client in the world, and she still would have left."

I dropped my head in my hands. "God, how did I get so screwed up?"

"You're not screwed up. And I do not blame you for being angry about not knowing about transferences, but now is the time when it's important to stick with the process. I know this is painful, but we're going in the right direction."

I picked up my keys and got up to leave.

"I want you to go back to the hospital tomorrow. I'm going to call Dr. Bryant and have him set up your psychodrama."

"What's a psychodrama?"

"It's a therapeutic experience to help you release some of these feelings. I think you're ready for it and you will be helping other people in the process."

I spent the rest of the day with the kids trying to make up for my long days at the hospital. Katie and Matthew were getting along better, only occasionally breaking into a battle of their preschool wit. After feeding the kids an early dinner, I went upstairs to our bedroom. Jeff walked in a few minutes later loosening his tie and unbuttoning his shirt. His face looked slightly pale and his body was a size smaller from weight loss. He lay down next to me on the bed and reached for my hand. I opened my palm and wove my fingers between his.

"I've been thinking," he said. "Should we press charges against your father? He shouldn't be able to just get away with this."

"I've thought about it too. But it's not worth it."

It was the height of the false-memories campaign, and the media was full of a few high-profile cases where adult daughters were accusing their fathers of child abuse. The defense was claiming that therapists were leading patients to believe they had been abused as a child and the parents were suing their children and therapists for what they had deemed were false memories. The process to seek legal justice was becoming as abusive as the abuse itself and neither one of us wanted to put our family through the ordeal.

I turned on my side and he spooned up against my back.

"Then I think I'll just kill him," he said. "If I plead insanity, I'll only have to go to prison for seven years."

"The kids would miss you too much," I said.

"Then I'll pay somebody to kill him for me."

"Still not worth it," I said. "Give this one to God."

"Is that what God's teaching you through all this?"

I sighed. "I have no idea what God's wants from me. I'm still too afraid to ask."

CHAPTER NINE

O n Wednesday our group entered the psychodrama building, a large room with stadium style seating that circled around an open stage. I sat between Patty and Liz while the adolescence from the inpatient side of the hospital entered the room. The boys dressed in sagging jeans and hoodie sweatshirts, the girls in over-sized T-shirts and leggings.

Dr. Bryant greeted the patients then gave a brief introduction about the therapeutic process. He explained that each of us would be affected by either participating or observing the reenactment of abuse and that whatever the scene triggered for us, we were then to go back to our groups and work through those issues.

He then walked over to where I was sitting and asked me to come up to the circle. I looked at Liz and she pushed me up by my lower back. Dr. Bryant then put his arm around my shoulders and walked me in a circle around the stage. My stomach felt as if I swallowed a rattlesnake, and I was waiting for it to strike.

"Dawn, can you tell the group a little bit about yourself?"

I slowly nodded. "I'm 33 years old, married, and I have three children."

"How old are your children?"

"Jen's 6, Matthew is 3, and Katie just turned 2."

"Sounds like a busy family. Can you tell us why you are in the program?"

I hated saying the word. "Incest. I was sexually abused by my father and some of his friends."

"Does any particular memory come up for you that you would like to deal with today?"

I closed my eyes and went with my first thought. "When I was five, my dad drove me into a canyon to punish me."

"How were you punished?"

"He raped me."

"Can you describe your father to the group? Tell us about his mannerisms and how you remember him that day." He kept his arm around me as we walked around the circle.

"He was gruff, his voice was low, angry."

"Could you pick out somebody in the room to play your father?" I scanned the seats. My eyes landed on a tall middle-aged man with a muscular body. I met him at lunch the previous day. He was a firefighter who entered the men's group after becoming debilitated by a sudden depression. I looked at him and he nodded his head, letting me know it would be okay to pick him. I called him up and he came to the center of the circle. The interns pulled out two chairs and arranged them side by side like the front seat of a car.

"Was your mother home at the time?"

"Yes. We were supposed to be going to the store. I didn't want to go with my dad but she said I had to."

"Could you pick out somebody to play your mother?" My eyes went to Liz. She looked like my mother with her short dark hair. They were both in their 50's and had a similar Southern accent. I told Liz that my mother had a stubborn, condescending way of dealing with me. She would make light of my concerns by laughing at me and supported my father as the benevolent dictator.

"Can you pick out some people to play your husband and your three children?"

I looked around the room and saw a Latino gang leader holding up his hand. He was as tall as Jeff, so I called him up. He high-fived his friend and came to stand next to me. My children were easy to select. Jen was played by a black girl who looked to be about 13 years old. The gentle spark that radiated from her eyes felt similar to the light I saw in Jen's. My son was played by a nine-year-old boy whose hair was as white as Matthew's, and I chose a teenager I often saw being supervised in the lobby outside of the cafeteria to play Katie.

Dr. Bryant and two other therapists prepared for the scene. They placed my father in one seat of the car and my mother standing outside of it. My children were in a huddle off to the side. The boy playing Jeff stood waiting for his cue.

The scene started with the voice of my father: "Get in the car, Dawn, we're going to the store."

My mother stood in front of me. "Now, Dawn, it's time to go to the store with your father. Go on now, get in the car."

I stood up to play my part, and as soon I did, it didn't feel like a role. I felt as if I was five years old, frustrated beyond words, frightened to leave the house with my father, sensing that if I did, I would somehow be terribly hurt.

"I don't want to go, Mom. I don't want to go."

"Dawn, get in the car. If your dad wants you to go with him, you go with him. He's the boss of this family and we do what he says."

I lost awareness of the room. My vocabulary was reduced to a child's.

"I don't want to go!"

"As long as you are under our roof, you will do what we say. Now get in the car!"

"Shut up, Mom! Shut up!"

"Don't you talk to me that way, I'm your mother!"

"You're so stupid! Stupid! Stupid!" I clenched my fist.

"Don't constrict your anger," Dr. Bryant said, "tell her everything you wanted to say." Two staff members came over and held a pillow between Liz and me.

"Hit the pillow," Dr. Bryant said.

"Dawn, your father's waiting. Get in the car."

"Can't you see what he's doing to me? Can't you?"

"You're going with him, Dawn. Get in the car."

I began to hit the pillow. The force of my punches were pulling my feet off the ground. "Mom, he's going to hurt me. Stop him! Don't make me go!"

"Dawn, that's nonsense. Your father would never hurt you."

"Get in this car," my father said.

"No. Please, no. I don't want to go. Please... Mom, don't make me, please."

"We're your parents. We know what's best for you, and you'll do what we say."

"Get in this car," said the raised voice of my father.

"I hate you, Mom! I hate you!"

She laughed at me. "Dawn, you're just going to the store. Now get in the car."

"I hate you forever and ever," I cried.

I sat in the seat next to my father. He slid next to me and put his hand on my thigh. I jumped out of my seat and danced around frantically.

"Don't touch me! Don't touch me!" I lurched toward my mother. The two therapists held me back.

"Hit the pillow."

I yanked my arm from their embrace and hit the pillow with a vengeance. Liz stayed in character; badgering me until my knees buckled and I started to sob.

"Mom," the young black woman's voice softly rose from the side of the room.

"It's Jen, Mom. I'm here and I need you."

I went from a five-year-old to a helpless mother.

"I'm so sorry, Jen. I'm so sorry." A sob erupted inside of me that burned like a torch through my body.

The girl playing Jen stepped forward. "I love you, Mom. I need you to help me grow up. Please, Mom, please come home where you belong."

The Latino boy playing Jeff came up and softly wiped my tears. His touch was so gentle. His eyes welled in tears as he pulled me into his arms. "It's over," he said. "I love you. I'm here to protect you, and nobody can hurt you again."

I broke down in his arms. The adolescents playing Matthew and Katie came up and embraced me. "We love you, Mom. We love you." We all stayed in the embrace, crying, until the therapists came over and walked us back to our seats.

My body was still trembling when I sat down, but my heart was full. The affection I received from the teenagers who played my children was so real, so honest, I wanted to take them all home.

Dr. Bryant then led an open forum where anybody could share what came up for them. The teens were active in the discussion. Many shared stories of abuse by a parent and how hopeless it made them feel. The boy that played Jeff, commented that it felt better to protect a family instead of a gang. His face was more relaxed than when I first saw him, and as he spoke his gentler nature could be felt throughout the room. The last patient to share was the girl that played Jen.

"It felt good to have a mother that cared about me," she said. "Even if she wasn't really my mom."

The teenagers became a part of us that day. Or maybe they always were. Like a bed of mud splattered diamonds, we all seemed to be reflecting common hues.

I drove home that evening feeling lighter, less burdened by anger I didn't realize I had. My breath was even starting to feel deeper. When I pulled into the driveway, Jeff was playing with the kids in the street. I was excited to share the experience with him, but he rushed off to a basketball game before we had a chance to speak.

I fed the kids, gave them a bath and then crawled in bed with Katie. A few minutes later, Matthew and Jen jumped in on either side. We all fell asleep entangled in a hug and woke up the next morning in the same position.

I was completing my last week at the hospital and felt like a different person. My protective walls were being dismantled one brick at a time and what was behind my inner construct continued to surprise me.

The security of our group would have been difficult to leave except that a new patient was admitted on Friday and by Monday the dynamic of the group had changed, and we were all rolling our eyes.

Her name was Kathy, a preppy-looking thirty-year-old who had all the answers and none of the problems. By her second day in the group, she had mentioned her master's degree in psychology thirty-seven times. Her response to a question was buried somewhere in a lengthy description of a lesson she taught to a Sunday school class. And if she told me what sorority she was an alumna of one more time, I would have been ready to knock her out. By Wednesday, I couldn't stand to sit through another group with her. I went to the hospital early and caught Dr. Bryant before our session. I followed him into his office. "What's going on?" he asked as he offered me a seat.

"This new woman, Kathy. She's driving me crazy. I can't stand to be in the same room with her."

Dr. Bryant got up and shut the door.

"Is this transference or something?" I asked.

"Transferences are when you transfer your feelings from one person onto another. Like how you have transferred feelings about your mother and father onto Anne. She was the person or source that is allowing you access to identify unresolved emotions from your childhood. But, I don't think that's what's happening here."

"Then what is happening?"

"What causes a situation like what you are experiencing with Kathy is called projection."

"What's that?"

"Projection is when we project feelings or personality traits of our own onto other people."

"You mean this obnoxious, controlling woman is trying to show me something about myself?"

"I think so. You see, the people you have connected with in the room reflect a part of yourself you like. You have bonded through mutual, likable traits. The people in our lives like Kathy, whom we dislike or even hate, tend to show us parts of ourselves we don't want to acknowledge."

"Are you sure about that?"

"Dawn, if she wasn't amplifying a part of you that you dislike or have disowned, she wouldn't be able to upset your peace of mind to the extent that she has."

"How do I find out what the projection is?"

"Easy. Just write down what you find annoying about her. Then put it in the first person."

I went back to the group. It seemed to me that Kathy's input was calculated. Her responses told us little about the way she felt and instead were centered on how she wanted us to think of her as a person. I wrote on my note pad.

She's trying to control what we think of her.
I put the sentence in the first person.
I try to control what people think of me.
Ugh. I felt my chest deflate. After the session, I went back to Dr. Bryant's office.
"That was a humbling experience," I said.
"What's that?"
"I often base what I'm going to say on what I want other people to think of me. I try to prove that I'm intelligent or accomplished, instead of just being who I am."
Dr. Bryant nodded and asked me to sit down. "When you're trying to prove yourself, what is it you're looking for?"
"I guess I'm looking for acceptance."
"So, when Kathy is trying to impress the group by her accomplishments or perceived skills, what is she really looking for?"
"Acceptance." My eyes welled as my shoulders sunk in toward my body.
"When children grow up in an environment that is either too controlling, or at times out of control, they're not able to fully secure an identity. If we don't develop a strong sense of self, we become hungry for acceptance from others."
A tear rolled down my cheek. Dr. Bryant stood up and handed me a box of tissues.
"Dawn, Kathy wants people to see her the way she wants to see herself. I admit she's doing a song and dance in group, but it comes from a painful need."
"Please tell me my song and dance doesn't look as bad as hers."
"It depends on who is watching it. Kathy looks different to every person in that room, and so do you. That's the point. You can't control what people think of you. And even if you could, it wouldn't solve the problem."

"And the problem is what I think of myself?"

"Yes, and the thoughts about ourselves are really the only thoughts we can control."

I stood up slowly and wiped my eyes.

"Dawn, you already are all the things you try to be. If you can acknowledge your strengths and become secure with your identity you won't struggle to have them secured by others."

"I don't even have an identity anymore."

"You do, but before we can find what's real, we have to eliminate what isn't."

I returned to group the following morning. Kathy entered the room a few minutes later. I sat through the day without irritation. She was free to play her song and dance. I was free not to.

That Friday, I was released from the program and had my final session with Dr. Bryant. When I entered the small office, he was wearing a white golf shirt and tan pants, his short black beard always neatly trimmed. He smiled when I walked in, moved some books off a side chair and asked me to sit down.

"Do you feel any better than when you started the program?" he asked.

"I feel very different."

"I haven't heard you say much about your therapist. You still having issues with her leaving?"

"Yes, but now that I know about transferences, I think I can deal with it better."

"Tell me more."

"The feelings I had toward my parents went away right after the psycho-drama. But when I think of Anne, I start to feel betrayed, misused, and angry. It's like my relationship with her is a portal to access my childhood feelings."

"That's exactly right," he said as he handed me a release form to sign. "Then you understand how transferences and projections can get in the way of the truth?"

"Yes, but I still think my relationship with her had more to it than transferences and projections. There was something deeper about it."

He looked at me like I still believed in Santa Claus. "Dawn, therapists are like parents. We want them to love us, accept us, and at times we want to believe that we are the most important people in their lives. When you're in that state of mind, it's easy to misinterpret a relationship."

I signed the papers and walked through the grounds of the hospital to my car. Had I misinterpreted my relationship with Anne? Or was separating my truth from other people's opinions one of the more difficult challenges of my life?

I came home from the hospital and picked up the mail. On the top of the pile was a postcard.

Hi Dawn,

Enjoying life on a tiny island in South Thailand. Front of postcard shows our bungalows--very quiet, beautiful. Warm water, good snorkeling, weather perfect. Am trying to make plans to go to Australia in December and may not return until March.

Thinking of you and really hope you're doing well.

Love,
Anne

Weight lifted from my shoulders. She wouldn't be contacting me until March, which would give me more time to work through my feelings and figure out where they were really coming from. I took the postcard up to the loft and put it in the file with Anne's picture. There was no need for another reminder of her around my house. My feelings of loss were constant, my longings for her unabated.

CHAPTER TEN

I had never been one to give much stock to coincidences, but they were starting to become so uncanny that the path I was on was verging on the mystical. The next level of my healing seemed to appear just as I was ready for it.

Dr. Bryant called to check up on me the week after I left the hospital. He suggested that it would be a good idea to take a Yoga or Tai Chi class. He explained that muscle tension can hold in our feelings and perceptions, and he thought I would continue to work through the abuse memories, and the depression more quickly if I added some kind of bodywork.

"Do you know of anybody you recommend?" I asked before getting off the phone.

"There are several around town--just keep your eyes open."

The next day, after dropping Jen and Matthew off at school, Laura and I put Katie in the stroller and went for a walk down the bike path to the beach. The path ended onto thick white sand and to the north, in a tucked away little cove, there was an instructor in the middle of what looked to be a yoga class.

"That's so weird," I said to Laura. "A doctor just told me I should do bodywork."

"Well, you know what they say?"

"What?"

"When the student is ready, the teacher appears."

"That sounds like something written in a fortune cookie."

She laughed. "That is probably where I read it."

We walked closer and sat down in the sand as he directed three women into positions that were held for several minutes. Their knees were bent, and their arms were stretched out in front of them with palms facing the ocean. He encouraged the women to stretch their fingers to the point of trembling.

"When you start shaking," the instructor said, "try to stay with it as long as possible. The shaking allows the body to release the blocked energy."

The next posture was similar. The hands here held high over their heads with the palms flat and facing the sky. The women's legs began to tremble, and the older woman finally broke the pose.

When the class ended, we went up and introduced ourselves to the instructor. Russ was an attractive man in his early thirties, with fair skin and thick black hair combed straight back. He asked our names then told us he started his students with a series of exercises that were a combination of Tai Chi and yoga to help open the Chakra system.

"What's a Chakra?" I asked.

"You don't know what a Chakra is?" said Laura.

"Like you do?"

"They are centers in your body where energy flows," she said.

"That's right," said Russ. "Chakras are energy wheels that exist in seven different points on the spinal column and up through the crown of your head. The base or root Chakra is in your tail bone."

He stepped next to Laura and placed his hand several inches from her rib cage. There is a root chakra at the pelvic floor then one here at the sternum, one over the heart, the throat, between your eyes and the top of your head. Also known as the crown chakra, the connection to the divine. They spiral in the body and are responsible for distributing the life energy. You might also have heard the life force called Qi or Prana."

"I know my Qi," Laura said.

"They open energy through the body and the mind," Russ said. "It's great if you need to do any grieving work."

"What if you don't need to do grieving work?" asked Laura.

"You are always going to be healthier if you keep your Chakras open."

"They close?"

"Yes. The wheels are sensitive, and they react to emotions and stress. When they close most people become sluggish and fatigued. Even depressed."

As we spoke, a tall dark-haired woman in the class walked up to us. I knew from national media coverage that her name was Heather. Her sister had been brutally stabbed to death just two months ago, allegedly by her husband, a well-known celebrity football player. Laura tapped me on the side as soon as she recognized who she was while Heather began asking us questions about where we lived, and what we did. When she was confident that we were not reporters, her voice softened, and she invited us to join the class. She then introduced me to her mother. Her aging, grief-stricken face glanced in my direct then out to the ocean.

"We're here every morning at eight-thirty," said Heather "You are welcome to join us."

Laura looked at me nodding her head.

"Thank you," I said to Heather. "We'll come tomorrow and check it out."

Laura kept hitting my side as we walked away.

"Oh my God, don't you think that's weird?"

"No, not really."

"Have you seen all the pictures of her sister? The one that was stabbed to death outside her home. Your coloring, body structure, and thick eyebrows. You look just like her."

"I don't look that much like her."

"Yes, you do," she said as she helped me lift Katie's stroller off the sand. "Serious, I saw her once down at the beach playing with her two kids. I thought it was you. This ought to be interesting." She said as we pushed the stroller back up the hill.

𝔔

The holidays quickly approached, and Jeff was excited to socialize with friends and neighbors. A week before Christmas, we went to a party up the street. It was the first time I had been to a social event in over a year, and I wasn't looking forward to it. I pulled a black cocktail dress from the back of my closet. It now fit like an oversized night shirt, and I felt like a child playing dress-up as I stood in front of the mirror brushing make-up on my cheeks. I threw on a red scarf and a long silver necklace and went downstairs to meet Jeff.

"How do I look?" I asked as we stood in the entry.

"Different."

"Different? That's never good."

"You look softer. Kinder."

He came up and put his arms around my waist. "Like you are more comfortable in your own skin."

"I might be more comfortable in my skin, but I don't think I'm going to be comfortable in a crowd."

"You don't have to stay. I will walk you home whenever you want to leave."

I welled up in tears. "I feel so raw. Like I don't have any shields to protect me."

"Well without shields, you are stunning."

We arrived at the party just past eight and most of the guests had already arrived. My heart started to pound as we came closer to the door. I felt like a walking open wound, a woman without a social identity to protect me. So much of me had melted away, I wasn't sure how I would relate to others.

Jeff opened the door and we entered. The living room looked like a small ballroom with guests dressed in black dresses and bright Christmas sweaters. The room echoed with holiday laughter, ice cubes chiming in tall cocktail glasses, the air smelling of perfume and cigars. The host, a loud ex-football player who made Jeff look like an average sized man, greeted us at the door. The men went into their stories about hunting while gravity seemed to pull me against the wall. I slowly stepped toward a clearing just outside the bathroom when Cynthia and another woman from our neighborhood flanked me like bookends.

"How are you feeling?" Cynthia asked in her tailored black dress and blinding diamond earrings.

My tongue felt thick and heavy I could barely push out the words. "I'm fine." The two women began to share stories about their children while I struggled to find my center, a sense of identity, a role to position myself so I could, at least, interact.

I made my way to the bar and drank a half a glass of wine, hoping it would take the edge off, or put one on. Instead, it sank me into a feeling of sadness and all I wanted to do was go home. I found Jeff out on the patio smoking cigars with some friends. I pulled him aside to say goodbye.

"Are you okay? Do you need me to walk you home?"

"No. I'm just tired. And I don't think I'm ready for a party yet."

He put his jacket over my shoulders, and I left alone to walk home. When I got to the curb, I saw Laura, her auburn hair falling off the shoulders of her long black coat.

"Where are you going?" she asked as she hugged me.

"I have to get out of here. This isn't me anymore."

"Come on. I'll walk you home," she said as she nodded to her husband to go into the party.

We walked down the street and around the corner to my house.

"I don't even know who I am anymore," I said.

She put her arm around my shivering shoulders. "You're a great mom, wife, and friend, and you will always be one hell of a businesswoman. Nobody can take those things from you. Not even your father."

"I don't feel like a very good wife these days. Not sure I ever was."

"Don't underestimate yourself. You keep him grounded. Can you imagine what he'd be like without you?"

"Maybe he would be better off."

"No. He'd just find some other emotionally unavailable woman to take care of him."

It felt good to laugh. We ran out of the cold and into my house. She checked on the kids with me and offered to stay.

"No," I said. "Go back to the party. You're dressed too nice to hang around here."

When Laura left, I laid down with the kids on the couch. We watched Disney movies until we all fell asleep. Jeff came in sometime after midnight. He fumbled up the stairs, reeking of gin and cigars as he entered our bedroom. He was now drinking as much as he did during his fraternity years in college, and as much as I hated the way it slowed his mind and dulled his eyes, I also felt it somehow compensated for what I couldn't give him. I turned over in bed and pretended to be asleep.

In the morning, I awoke to his chest against my back. It was Saturday and the kids were still asleep.

"I'm lonely," he said as his hand caressed my thigh. "I don't want to pressure you, but I need to feel like you want me."

"I'm sorry. It's not that I don't want you... it's just that I can't be with you right now."

He turned me over on my back, his blue eyes fixed on mine. "I didn't do this to you, and I feel like I'm being blamed for it."

I couldn't answer. He dropped his head back on the pillow. "Then there's only one thing left for me to do," he said.

"What's that?"

"It's time to find a girlfriend." He jumped out of bed and put on his clothes.

"A girlfriend. You're really going to go find a girlfriend?"

"A man's got to do what a man's got to do."

He grabbed his keys off the nightstand. "I'll see you in a couple hours."

I laid back on my pillow, curious but not worried. If he was really looking for a girlfriend, I doubt he would have announced it to me.

At noon, his car pulled up and the kids and I walked out to greet him.

"Come on," he said as he grabbed my hand, "I want you to meet the new woman in my life." He opened the door to the van and an 18-month-old black Labrador retriever jumped out and licked me.

"They didn't have any females left at the humane society, so she is really he and his name is Maxx."

Maxx jumped all over me, as starved for affection as Jeff was.

"So, Maxx, you're my new competition?"

Jeff came up and hugged me. "Maxx and I will wait for you for as long as we have to."

I melted in his arms. There was such a sweetness to Jeff. And, when it came out, he was irresistible to me. That day, more than ever, I wanted to be through with the journey so that I could love Jeff the way I knew Maxx would.

The new year was feeling ominous. We put the company up for sale with a business broker while the economy, and the number of our clients, continued to decline. I wondered if it would sell before we had to shut the doors. Jeff and I didn't talk about that scenario, instead we stayed optimistic that what we built together was still of value.

In the meantime, I walked the yellow brick road that was paved with uncanny experiences. My latest direction came from a book, *The Tibetan Book of Living and Dying*, that a friend had given me for Christmas. I resisted reading anything that had death or dying in the title but this one beckoned me like a magnetic pull every time I passed it on the nightstand. One night, as the light from the nightstand glistened off the airtight seal, I thought I should at least open it and put it in the bookshelf. Oddly though, when I pierced the packaging, I suddenly found myself enveloped by a sense of falling in love with the book. Enchanted by the experience, I opened the cover and began to read. Shortly after, I found my message:

> *When we have prayed and aspired and hungered for the truth for a long time, for many, many lives, and when our karma has become sufficiently purified, a kind of miracle takes place. And this miracle, if we can understand and use it, can lead*

to the ending of ignorance forever: The inner teacher, who has been with us always, manifests in the form of the "outer teacher," whom, almost as if by magic, we actually encounter. This encounter is the most important of any lifetime.

Who is the teacher? None other than the embodiment and voice and representative of our inner teacher. The master whose human shape and human voice and wisdom we come to love, with a love deeper than any other in our lives, is none other than the external manifestation of the mystery of our own inner truth. What else could explain why we feel so strongly connected to him or her?

For thousands of years it had been a Tibetan practice to place a student with a teacher until the student saw his own soul in the eyes of the teacher. The divine reflection was the nature of the mind, the Buddha, the Christ within, the divine spark of our own soul. I thought about the message I received. When I saw Anne's soul, I would see my own. I felt like I found the answer to the riddle. It was a known practice that helped me finally make sense of why I felt so strongly about her.

I quickly flipped through the book looking for a passage that would describe how the student went about seeing the soul of the teacher. The blessing was usually given to the student from the teacher in person. But, if the teacher was not present with the student, the author suggested reflecting on a picture.

I jumped up from the bed and walked to the loft to take out Anne's picture, amazed she was moved to give it to me, knowing she had no idea that I would need it to reflect my soul. I sat down at my desk and pulled out the photograph. It felt good to see her face. I could now feel my feelings for her deep inside my heart. My capacity to love her was so much greater than when she had left.

I brought the book to my next session with Judith and told her about the experience. She put on her glasses and read the passage, her reaction as dry as the arrant winter air that surrounded her office.

She closed the book and handed it back to me. "From a psychological perspective," she said, "this sounds like a projection. When your mind is ready, you project your own compassion or Christ-like nature onto somebody else."

"Then how come I didn't project it onto you, or anybody else in my life?"

"I think Anne was just the first person you truly trusted."

I set down the book on the coffee table. "You really know how to suck the grace right out of this."

"I'm sorry, but I believe there are a range of people you could have had the same experience with."

"So, if I had met you first I would have had this experience with you?"

"It would have been a different path, but I believe it would have taken you to the same place."

I shook my head. "Judith, I met Anne first for a reason. She brought back a piece of me. A piece that I lost in my own reflection. Anne showed me what I really look like."

"I believe that's true. I just don't think this has anything to do with Anne."

"It has everything to do with Anne. What was in her, is in me too. I am just not connected to it yet. I'm still cut off from my own compassionate Christ-like nature. But I can see it in her, and that's why I love her so deeply."

"But she's also a human being who walks the face of this earth. She has her own problems and issues just like everyone else."

"Believe me, I know, and I'm sober about this. Anne has qualities that I feel are stronger than mine, but I have many qualities that I feel are stronger than hers. Judith, I'm not supposed to worship her. I'm just supposed to love her."

Judith asked to see the book again and opened to the passage. "Dawn, the teacher they refer to in this book is an enlightened master. I think Anne has the potential to be enlightened, but I do not consider her to have been at that level of consciousness when she left here."

"Neither do I, but I see something in her that goes beyond her personality, beyond her fears and awkwardness."

She looked down at the book again and shook her head. "I knew Anne fairly well, and when I read this I have to wonder, which one of you is the teacher and which one of you is the student."

I was warmed by her words, but the sentiment seemed irrelevant. "I haven't looked at it that way," I said. "But the setup when we started was that she was the teacher."

"Well, I wouldn't get hung up in that setup, especially at the rate that you process."

"I don't think that's the point. Her picture connects me to my soul and this relationship is helping me release the negative feelings about myself that are preventing me from connecting to who I really am, and what it is I'm being called to do."

"But according to this book, the practice only works if the person you are using as a mirror is an enlightened master."

"Then why did I have that reaction to the book? I was filled with love before I even opened it. And what about Anne's picture? Giving a client a picture is a highly unusual gesture, and I think it's a pretty powerful coincidence."

Her expression remained skeptical.

"Do you think Anne is conscious of any of this?"

"No, I'm sure she's not, but something moved her. She had no idea why she was giving me that picture, but it was important to her that I have it."

She shrugged. "Well, I don't see where looking at her picture is going to hurt you. You might as well give it a try." Her lack of conviction was frustrating. I wanted Judith to believe in my path as much as I needed to, but that wasn't going to happen; boom or bust, I had to believe in me and continue to have faith in my direction.

It was raining when I came home from Judith's office. Our three-car garage no longer had room for a car. Jeff bought a used pool table that took up half the room and he'd converted the other half into an office he planned on using when the company sold. I jumped out into the rain and slipped through the side door. Jeff was building a mud volcano with Matthew for a school project while Maxx lay next to them watching.

"How was your session?" he asked.

"It was okay." I thought about telling him about the message in the Tibetan book, but even I thought it was strange to be looking at her picture, so I decided to keep it to myself.

§

Three times a week, Laura and I would go to the beach for our Tai Chi sessions with Russ, and for ten minutes a night I would look at Anne's photo. I'm not sure what the practice was doing to me, but my path, once turbulent, was now an exorcism. Memories of my father and the abuse from him and his friends continued as did all the body sensations that came with them. It was as if everything I once numbed myself to feel was now dethawing, waking up cells in my body that had been dormant for decades. At night my dreams were drenched with emotions: the horror of drowned children, the loss of control to a fatal disease. I dreamt of Anne leaving me with the apathy of a stranger. Hours later, I dreamt of forcing my father at gunpoint to admit to my family what he had done to me.

Jeff was starting to notice that things had intensified. I would toss and turn at night, wake up in a sweat and then leave the room so he could go back to sleep. One night before bed he walked into the loft while I was looking at Anne's picture. When he entered, I slid the photo back into my journal.

"Do you want to take Maxx out with me?" he asked. "The fresh air might help you sleep better."

"I'd love to."

We walked out to the backyard and climbed in the hammock while Maxx chased wild rabbits into the canyon.

"I notice you keep looking at her picture," he said. "Should I be worried about that?"

"No, I don't think so." I told him about the practice I learned in *The Tibetan Book of the Living and Dying* and that I was using her picture to help me bring back a part of myself. "The book was kind of a sign," I said.

"Like a lobster buoy," he said as he pulled me closer into his chest.

"Like a lobster buoy?"

"Ever since this started with you, I kept praying for a sign and suddenly all these lobster buoys began to appear. I used to never find them, and now I see them all the time." He pointed to the fence that was lined with rows of colorful buoys tied together with fishing wire. "See how many I have collected this year. Most of the time, I swim out to get them.

They get stuck on a reef or seaweed after the fisherman pick up their lobster traps. But this past week, Maxx and I found one right on the beach."

"What do you make of that?" I asked.

"God's looking out for us. As long as I keep finding lobster buoys, I know wherever all this leads, it's going to be okay."

I squeezed his big barrel chest. As difficult as it was for both of us, I somehow knew it was all going to be okay too.

✺

It was the end of March and every time I looked at Anne's picture it seemed like she was nearby, as if she was just up the street. I couldn't shake the feeling until one night Judith called to change the time of our next appointment to earlier in the day. Before we got off the phone, I shared with her that it felt like Anne was in town. There was a long pause after I spoke.

"She was here," she said. "I was waiting for our next session to tell you."

"What do you mean, was?"

"She was home for a couple of weeks. She took off again yesterday."

"What! Why didn't she call me?" I asked.

"I don't know."

"Did she ask about me?"

Another long pause. "No. I'm sorry, she didn't."

Her answer knocked the breath out of me.

"Do you know where she went or when she's coming back?"

"She moved. She packed up her stuff and took it somewhere up north. I think she was going to keep traveling."

"Judith, I went into the hospital the day she left. Doesn't she even want to know how I am?"

"She's going through a divorce right now. I wouldn't take her actions personally."

"Is she alright?"

"She's fine. Anne knows how to take care of herself."

I stared down at her picture sitting in my open journal. "I can't believe she didn't ask about me."

"I'm sorry. I have some time tomorrow if you want to come in and talk about it."

"No," I said as tears rolled down my cheeks. "I think I just need to sit with this for a minute."

We hung up the phone and I floored myself in the loft for the rest of the night. How could she return and not call me? Not even ask about me? The one I trusted. The one I thought understood and loved me. As the lights went out in the house, my tears turned into quiet sobs. My heart was broken and bleeding. Intense feelings of rejection and abandonment waved over me like a relentless sea as the faces of Anne and my parents reeled across my mind. For the rest of the night, I rolled up in a blanket and sobbed in anguish until I couldn't breathe. With my stomach aching from the convulsions, my body completely exhausted from tears, I lay back on the floor and watched through the window as a brilliant pink sky turned to a clear powder blue. My emotions were drained, my thoughts had emptied, and from the blank slate in my mind a message arose.

Love is not what you receive from others;
it's what you have for them.

A smile slowly came to my face. In that still moment, lying alone on the cold floor, in a blanket soaked with my tears, I realized the love that I thought was dependent on others was something I already had. It was a part of me that couldn't leave--the part of me I felt when I thought of the people I loved. Love was my own experience, and as Jen once tried to teach me, the more you try to give love away, the more it comes right back at ya.

Jeff seemed to be soothed by his love affair with Maxx. They ran on the beach each morning, always bringing back a stick, a feather, or a washed-up lobster buoy. In the evening they wrestled in the yard and rolled on the grass, chewing on each other's ears. I sat up in the loft and watched them out the window. They were both so present with each other. I wondered if I would ever be so enlightened.

I wanted to contact Anne, but I knew it wasn't right, so I focused my energy on the book. The message to *tell the story* often came to me in the early morning, but I had no idea what the story was, so I continued to look for one.

I picked up a stack of books at the library about psychology, philosophy, and writing. The reading took me out of my misery. Or at least I thought it did--until my mother called.

"Before I come up and see the kids again," she said in her southern drawl, "I would like to talk to you about a few things."

"What do you have in mind?"

"Oprah Winfrey had a show on yesterday about false memories. Did you see it?"

"No, but I've heard about this before."

"Well, I think you should hear it again, because it's happening all over the country. These women on her show had been led in therapy to believe they had been sexually abused by their fathers."

"Mom, I've never been led in therapy, and if you're concerned that I have, why don't you and Dad come up and see my therapists?"

"The only person I want to talk to is Anne Myers."

It was a safe command. She knew Anne had been gone for months.

"This has nothing to do with Anne. I've remembered more abuse memories since seeing other therapists than I ever did with Anne."

"She's the one who made the original diagnosis and she's the only person I want to talk to."

"There was no diagnosis, and it's not possible to see Anne. You're welcome to come up and see Judith."

"Dawn, you and Anne Myers accused your father of abusing you and then she leaves the country. What kind of therapist is that? And where is she now? Where is she when I want to talk to her?"

"You had six months to talk to her between the time I told you about the memories and the time Anne left on vacation."

"Then when is she coming back?"

"She's not. She moved."

She started to laugh, and I started to cry.

"How do you know she didn't suggest your father abused you while you were under some kind of hypnosis?"

"I was never unconscious."

"You don't know that!"

"Yes, I do!" Why was I still on this phone?

She took a breath and reloaded. "If your father was hurting you, why would you go with him? Why would you let him do that to you?"

"I was a child!" I said as I raised my voice. "What else was I supposed to do?"

"You could have told me."

"I tried to. Remember the time in the bathroom?"

"That could have been a coincidence."

I cleared my throat so she wouldn't hear me crying. "Mom, come have a therapy session with Judith and me and we will discuss this further."

"No. I'm not going to do that. Your father said we have to be very careful about what we say or do. He thinks you might press charges."

I slammed down the phone.

My faith in humanity dissolved. My parents' protecting themselves against the legal system had become more important than feeling compassion for their own daughter.

୨

The company sold that June. By the end of August, we were closing down the building and helping the employees transfer into the new corporation.

The day we were to hand the keys back to the landlord, I drove to the office with Jeff to sign off on the lease. A strange mood of fear and relief hung in the air as Jeff and I talked about the logistics of the sale and avoided any conversation about what we would do next, or how we would live when the money from the acquisition ran out.

Jeff opened the door as we entered the two-story steel and glass building. An office that once bustled with fast-paced activity was now an empty cavern. Our footsteps echoed through the building as Jeff walked out to the warehouse to meet the landlord and I walked upstairs and into my office. A layer of dust outlined where my desk once stood, and the only thing left in the room was a small box. I walked over and slowly picked it up. Inside was a picture of the kids covered in sand at the beach, a gold plaque awarding me *Woman Entrepreneur of the Year*, and a smooth rock engraved with the word Trust that one of our employee's had given me several years ago. I held the rock in my hand knowing it too was a message. Every circumstance I was living seemed to have meaning, and my challenge was to decode it. Find out what the moment was asking of me, and how to participate in it fully, so like a video game, I could advance to a higher level.

I found Jeff that night in the garage cutting out the inside of an old cargo van from the office and building what looked like a bed across the back. I walked in when he was halfway through the project.

"What are you making?" I asked.

"A dog van," as he revved up his power drill.

"What for?"

"When we receive the check for the company next week, Maxx and I are going on a fishing trip."

"For how long?"

He turned off the drill. "Indefinitely."

"Excuse me?"

"Indefinitely." He leaned up against the van. "For the past 2 years, I've taken care of your company, the kids, and you. Now it's time I take care of myself."

"Where are you going?"

"I'm heading north. You can meet me in Idaho for the wedding, then I'll probably go into the Sierras for a while."

I had forgotten about the wedding. Jon, one of our best friends from high school was getting married in a small town in Idaho in just a few weeks.

"When are you coming home?"

"I don't know. But every time you ask me, the trip is going to get longer."

I leaned up against his workbench and looked at him. On any given day, Jeff was either loving and supportive or petulant and belligerent. But I was starting to understand him more. We were both orphans with similar wounds that found different expressions. Jeff had never worked through the feelings around his father's death, and my hope was that his trip would give him time for his own healing.

Jeff left early that fall, the day after the kids started back to school. I dropped them off in their classrooms and met Laura at the beach for Tai Chi. Heather and her mom showed up a few minutes late. I had seen them on a national interview the night before, and as busy as they were with the upcoming trial, I was glad they were still finding time to come to the beach. Russ led us through the first several exercises then he put us in positions and asked us to hold the pose for long periods of time. When we did my limbs would tremble. As my muscles fatigued, feelings would come up in my chest like storm clouds. Mostly sadness and shame. I looked over at Heather and saw tears running down her face and suddenly the clouds in my chest got denser.

We moved to another position. Our arms straight over our heads and our fingers were spread out as far as possible. My eyes were fixed on the blue horizon, the waves pounding onto shore, while feeling the strong presence of Heather next to me and her mother next to her. We went to the next position, our arms held out at shoulder length, our fingers spread out and pointing to the sky.

I heard a child's yell and suddenly two young boys ran up from behind us. "Hey, Grandma!" they said as they threw their towels on the sand and ran down to the water. One of the boys was the son of the daughter who had been recently murdered. I didn't recognize the other. We went to the next position as I watched her grandson play in the waves. The water glistening off his black skin made me wonder if the ocean soothed his heart the way it used to soothe mine. He dove under a wave then slowly emerged, perhaps hoping that pushing through the surface of the water would somehow wake him from his tragic nightmare.

When class was over Heather walked up to me, "let me introduce you to my son and nephew." She called the kids up from the water and I tensed as the five-year-old boy approached us. I remember Laura telling me that I looked like his mother, and I was concerned that my presence might startle him.

Before I could excuse myself, he saw me standing next to his aunt and grandmother on the same beach where he often came with his mother. My long, blonde hair was enough to give him hope, and from a hundred feet away we locked eyes--seeing something strangely familiar in him, him desperate to see his mother in me, I wanted to say 'I'm sorry I'm not her,' but his mind was already caught in the confusion. As he marched toward me, I could see his hope turn to sadness, then a rage that brought tears to us both. I wasn't who he needed me to be. He quickly turned away and raced back into the water.

I walked into my session with Judith that afternoon still haunted by the experience. I put my keys down and dropped into the couch as I explained to her what happened at the beach.

"I'll never forget his face," I said.

"What did you see in him?"

The torment in his dark brown eyes was still etched in my mind. "He's holding his breath. Deep in his heart, he's holding his breath, waiting for his mother to return."

She stared at me. "Who are you holding your breath for?"

My stomach slowly sank to the floor. "I hate it when you do that," I said.

"You didn't answer the question."

I looked down thinking about the boy. "When you're a child, you hope. You hope that someday the people who have left your life will reappear, love you the way you need to be loved, and everything that happened will fade like a terrible dream."

"And what happens if you stop holding your breath? If you let go of the hope?"

"I'll die. If I give up the hope, I can't survive."

"You can't survive," she leaned forward, "or the five-year-old child inside of you can't survive?"

"Both."

"Are you still waiting for Anne to return?"

"I know it doesn't make sense but waiting for Anne to return goes much deeper than Anne. I'm waiting for a part of me to return, and I have to believe, I have to hope that someday that's going to happen."

"And what if it doesn't? What if, just like that little boy, you have to realize that she's never coming back?"

"Then I don't know what will happen to me."

"Dawn, you took Anne for your mother. And there is no hope that she will ever be your mother. You need to realize that."

"I know she wasn't my mother, but the need for her is still so strong."

"Because it's an old need and that need will eventually go away. And when it does, I think you will connect to the part of you that you truly miss."

"It doesn't feel like it's ever going to go away."

Judith sat back in her chair. "Close your eyes," she said.

"Why?"

"Just do it."

I was too tired to protest so I closed my eyes and took a deep breath.

"I want you to go to your garden and ask a child to appear. When you have someone, let me know."

I entered the wood garden gate and found two children sitting on the white bench. The first child was me as a five-year-old, still wearing my black turtleneck and blue jeans, sitting with one knee up under her arm. The second was me at the age of eight. My permanent teeth had come in, and my bangs were cut an inch above my eyebrows. I gave Judith the description.

"The five-year-old looks lonely and the eight-year-old is scared, distant."

"Ask them why they feel that way."

"The five-year-old needs Anne. She wants somebody safe to love. And the eight-year-old is afraid. She is still afraid the men are going to kill her."

Judith cleared her throat. "Dawn, I want you to bring yourself into the image as an adult and take the two children in your lap. When they're comfortable I want you to show them a photo album. Show them pictures of Jeff, Jennifer, Matthew, and Katie. Show the five-year-old all the people in her life that she can safely give her love to. And then show the eight-year-old pictures to let her know she grew up. She's safe now; the men didn't kill her."

I took the two children in my lap and opened the photo album. But the first picture that appeared, was the picture the men showed me. The Polaroid of the dead girl lying naked on the floor, her throat slit from ear to ear. My heart started to race and my hands sweated profusely.

"Judith, it's the picture my dad and his friends showed me of the dead girl. It was what was going to happen to me if

I told anybody. These men are going to kill me. I'm not safe! I'm not safe anywhere!"

"You're all right and you're safe. Tell me what you're experiencing."

I started to cry. "The child in this picture was killed. She was murdered." I felt the terror she felt before her death, the terror I numbed out when they threatened my life by holding the picture in front of me.

I opened my eyes and jumped to my feet. "They're going to kill me. I knew too much. I played along so they wouldn't hurt me, but I still knew too much." I paced the floor and waves of fear sent chills up my body. "I never knew when they were going to change their minds. When they had had enough of me. I never knew when they were going to kill me."

"Dawn, they didn't kill you. You grew up. It's over."

"It's never over!" I yelled as I pounded my fist on the door. "It's inside of me every single day!"

Judith was silent.

I sat back down on the couch and held a pillow to my chest. "Why did my dad do this to me? Damn him! I'm not going to be safe until he's dead. Until I kill him before he kills me."

"How would you kill him?"

"With a shotgun."

Judith pulled out a box of crayons and a large pad of paper.

"Come sit on the floor. Pick out a crayon and draw me a picture of your father."

I pulled out a thick red crayon that looked like blood and drew a stick figure of my dad.

"Now draw the gun," she said. I drew a stick figure of myself pointing a shotgun in his face. "You've got the gun to his head. What do you want him to say to you?"

"I'm sorry. I want him to acknowledge what he did and say he's sorry."

"Write it."

I drew a line from his mouth. In big, red letters I wrote: *I'M SORRY, DAWN. I'M SORRY!*

"What do you want to do next?"

"Kill him."

"Then kill him." I took my red crayon and crossed him out of my life like the death of a bad dream. When his picture was nothing more than a blotch of red wax, I doubled over and sobbed.

"He's dead, Dawn. He can't hurt you anymore."

I gasped for air. "I love you, Dad. I love you."

CHAPTER ELEVEN

The phone rang and Katie ran to pick it up. The caterer was calling to get a final head count for the wedding. I went into my office and pulled up the list from my computer.

"107," I said as I walked back to the kitchen table. She relayed the message and hung up the phone.

"Geez, Mom. I had no idea the therapy you were in was so intense."

"It was intense."

"And I can't believe Heather and her mom lived by us. I recently saw a documentary on the murder. He just got out of jail."

"Yes, he did."

"Do they still live by the beach?"

"I don't think so. I have seen Heather a few times at fundraisers to stop domestic violence but after the day when I saw the boy, they stopped coming to the Tai Chi class. Russ said it was because the trial was starting soon. I hoped that was the only reason."

Katie shook her head. "Matthew and Jen just referred to that time as Mom's depression. But it was so much more than that."

"It really was. You could feel it in the house. The depression was heavy, but there was also this thick intimacy that hung in the air like we were being protected in a cocoon, watched over by forces we couldn't see. Isabella used to call it the *llamda spiritual*. The calling of the spirit. None of us knew where it was leading but we all knew it was leading to something."

"Was Isabella freaked out by any of it?"

"No. She's so sturdy. Honestly, I think she was a God send. She came to live with us just before this started to happen."

"I love Isabella," she said.

"So do I."

She stood up and took her wine glass to the sink. "When did the abuse stop? How old were you?"

"It ended when I was around 8 years old. My dad got ill and very thin. He was sick to his stomach most of the time. It lasted for years, and the doctors could not determine what was wrong with him. By the time he got better, I was in junior high."

"He deserved to get sick. And, to go to jail."

I nodded. Katie looked out the window as the lights began to twinkle across the town. "Can I spend the night?" she asked. "I want to hear how this ends."

"I'd love for you to stay."

"Do you still have one of Dad's big shirts?"

I smiled. "There is one in the nightstand downstairs. Bottom draw on the left."

Katie ran downstairs to shower and change while I responded to emails to confirm a few more wedding details. When she came back to the living room, I poured us some hot tea. Jeff's white tee-shirt still hung on her like a night gown. Her long thick-red-hair now flowing more than half-way down the shirt. We sat down on the sectional couch and wrapped blankets around our feet.

"Was this all leading toward the messages?"

"Yes. And it was so uncanny. Everything that was happening in my life seemed to be so intelligently organized to help me heal, and then receive. I had to just keep moving through the feelings."

"What feeling was the hardest?"

"By far, the most difficult was shame."

"Shame?"

"Yes. It's our greatest obstacle. I have come to learn that we all have some version of a that wound. It's like a belly button from being cast out of the womb, expelled from the great mother. But when you have been abused, neglected, or oppressed the wound is larger, more sensitive, and it makes it very difficult to believe you are lovable and worthy. Let alone significant enough to be summoned to a deity."

"I can't wait until we get to that part," she said as she snuggled into the couch.

After Heather and her mom left Tai Chi, Laura and I still went to class at the beach.

Russ told me one morning that my heart Chakra was closed. I wasn't sure how he knew that, but since Jeff left on his trip my energy was low and my emotions were becoming more intense. Holding the positions that morning just seemed to make me feel worse.

I went in to see Judith the next day.

"Whatever God is calling me to do, better be good," I said as I plunged down in the tapestry chair, "because I am sick to death of this suffering."

She smiled. "What's going on?"

"Sucky black feelings are going on."

"What are the feelings about?"

I closed my eyes for a moment to find the words. Then thought about whether I wanted to say them out loud.

"Don't worry," Judith said. "They are just feelings."

"Okay." I stared toward the corner of the room. "I feel like there is something disgraceful or repulsive about me that I have always needed to cover up. And, I'm afraid when people get too close to me, intimately close to me, they see it."

"Give me an example."

I shifted in my seat. "I don't know if I have told you this, but the last day I saw Anne, she held me in her arms for most of the session. I was so raw and vulnerable with her. I had never let anybody close enough to me to hold me like that, and afterwards it embarrassed me."

"How so?"

"When my walls were down, when Anne had the chance to see me for who I am, I think she saw something very ugly. Something so disgraceful that she didn't want to see me again."

Judith winced. "You're describing shame. The feeling that at the core of our being we are ugly and undesirable."

"Ugly, worthless, humiliated. Anne not staying in contact with me makes me feel the way I did when my dad molested me. He didn't want to talk to me either. I was so ugly it made him go away, and it feels like whatever my dad saw in me, Anne saw, too."

"That sounds very painful."

"It makes me so disgusted with myself, I want to leave my own body."

"Does Jeff leaving make you feel this way too?"

I suddenly felt worse. "It probably helped trigger it."

She nodded. "Do you understand that your vulnerability with Anne had nothing to do with her leaving? The shame you feel is the legacy your father, and the men he left you with, handed down to you. It's a feeling, but who you are is not your feelings of shame. You are not ugly, unworthy, or unlovable."

"I do understand that, " I said, "but knowing the truth seemed to only be the first stage of actually realizing it."

Judith nodded. "Do you know where you feel the shame in your body?"

"It starts in my sternum and goes to the seat of my pelvis."

"Do you want to do a guided meditation?"

The depth of my shame was the depth of my hell, and I wasn't all that eager to go there.

"Do I have to?"

She raised an eyebrow and grinned. "Close your eyes."

"You like this don't you?"

"Not as much as you think."

I took a deep breath and leaned my head back against the chair.

"Bring your awareness into the area you describe in your chest and when you have settled there for a moment, tell me what you see and feel."

As soon as I closed my eyes the image of the woman in the shawl appeared in my mind. Behind her was the Light, radiating like a summer sun.

Trust yourself and start writing.

I explained the images to Judith and repeated the inaudible message that came with the image.

"Okay. Stay with the image and tell me what else you notice."

After a few moments of silence, I felt a pull drawing me into a cave that opened at the center of my chest. The entrance was large and dark. A chill ran through my body and a seductive thirst pulled me more deeply into the cave.

Stop resisting, stop resisting.

I let go of my desire to stay at the entrance of the cave and felt the sensation of being sucked into its vortex. My body suddenly felt horizontal, as if I was lying flat on my back, buried alive in a six-foot grave.

"Judith, I'm in a grave."

"Dawn, ask the woman what this image is all about."

Let go. Let go of your life.

I repeated the message to Judith and told her I was fighting to dig myself out.

"Fight as long as you need to," she said. I struggled until I was exhausted. Knowing I couldn't get out, I finally gave up. A moment later, I felt myself return to the sensation of being horizontal. I looked around and saw that I was now on a small platform going down into a well. It was dark and stuffy, and the platform I was on suspended me at a level just above my sternum. I described the image to Judith.

"Dawn, ask the woman or the Light to tell you more about where you are."

I asked and repeated the words to Judith. "The grave shows me that I need to let go of my life. The well represents a new transition."

"Ask them what you need to do next."

Stay in the well. Be aware.

I repeated the message to Judith, then shot open my eyes and jumped up from my seat. "Do you think I'm really going to die?"

"Someday."

"I don't like this, Judith. It scares me."

"What scares you about it?"

"I'm on a platform that's going down into a well in my body, and I was just told to let go of my life. I don't want to let go of my life."

"I think it's just a metaphor. Throughout mythology you can see the process of transformation illustrated by the images of towers, caves, castles, and wells. It is in these dark, scary places that the hero enters to retrieve lost parts of themselves."

"But this well is in my body."

"I believe the well represents you dropping down into your feelings of shame and unworthiness. And beneath them, there is something very genuine about you that I believe will be discovered."

"If the process doesn't kill me."

She grinned. "Just remember what the woman told you--stay in the well and pay attention."

"Are you sure I'm not going to die?"

"I don't know. I left my crystal ball at home."

I winced in frustration. "You're not very comforting."

"You're in a well. I don't think you are supposed to be comfortable."

I sat back in my chair, hoping she'd say something soothing and compassionate, hoping she'd say something Anne would say. She didn't, so I stood up to leave.

"Judith, do you think I'm ever going to hear from Anne again?"

"I don't know, but if you don't, you shouldn't take it personally. How other people handle their relationships has nothing to do with you as a person. It's how they are in the world, and it's not about you."

"That's a hard one for me."

"That's a hard one for everyone."

I reached for the door.

"Just a minute," she said. "While you are in the well, there is something else I want you to do."

"What?"

"Write Anne's eulogy."

I shook my head. "I really don't want to do that, Judith. She is part of my process and it's helping me to access my feelings."

"I don't think you need her anymore to access your feelings."

She stood up from her chair. "I've talked to a few other therapists about it including Dr. Bryant. We all knew Anne. She is not coming back, and nobody really knows where she has gone. For your psychological well-being you need to have closure."

I wasn't ready to give up. But I was also starting to consider the possibility that seeing the reflection of my soul in Anne might not be a literal experience.

"I'll think about it," I said as I walked out the door.

When I pulled into the driveway a large letter "M" was written in blue crayon across the white garage door. I walked in the house and found Matthew in the family room watching a video. He was still in the jeans and red shirt he wore to school. On the floor next to him was a thick blue crayon.

"Matthew, did you draw the "M" on the garage door?" I asked.

He looked me right in the eye. "No, Mom, it wasn't me."

"Do you think Katie or Jen would have written a large 'M' on the garage door?"

"Maybe they were trying to write Mom," he said as he nonchalantly turned his head back toward the TV.

I thought for a moment how my mother would have ranted and screamed at me if I had done the same thing, or how quickly she would have jumped to the conclusion that I was to blame. I reached down and gently turned over the palm of his hand. There was a thin layer of blue wax covering his fingers.

"Let's go son," I said as I lifted him to his feet. "If you're going to tag," I said as I walked him out to the garage, "never use your own initials."

We filled up a bucket of water and soap and started sponging the crayon off the door.

"Mom, when's Dad coming back?" he asked, as he glided over the crayon marks making no effort to erase them.

"He'll be home in a couple of weeks."

"Is he bringing home any fish?"

"Probably."

He crunched his nose.

"Mom, I hate dead fish."

"I don't care for them much either," I said as I put his sponge-filled hand in mine and taught him how to clean crayon off a door.

I fed the kids and gave them a bath. We read stories in bed until one by one they fell asleep. The house was quieter without Jeff. The tension between us didn't linger in the air and being home felt more peaceful. The kids even seemed a bit calmer.

Once they were tucked in, I went into my room, picked up my journal and nestled into bed. I pulled out the photo of Anne. Looking at her picture was now bringing up intense layers of shame that made me realize I was descending deeper into the well. I sat with the feelings of shame and imbued in my self-disgust, was the embarrassment I felt for falling in love with a woman. Someone of my same sex, and the queasy look I imagined my mother would give me if she knew. My heart constricted. Maybe Judith was right. Perhaps it was time to end the relationship and kill Anne off in my mind too.

I grabbed a pen off the nightstand and started writing her eulogy. I wrote out a few awkward sentences. *Anne you were a trusted, loving, therapist…yuck.* I scratched out the words and tried again. After my third attempt, I tossed the journal on the floor and curled up in the blanket. Shortly after, I fell into a deep sleep and an even deeper dream.

In the dream, I walked out of a dark, cold night wearing a down-jacket into a small apartment. On a daybed in the living room sat Anne, wearing a soft pink sweater that extended to her ankles. A woman in her late fifties stood a few feet away. She had the medium round build of my mother, short, sassy salt-and-pepper hair, and harsh, black eyeliner that accentuated her pale skin and bitter eyes.

I locked eyes with Anne. Her soul was illuminated, her love much stronger than I had felt in real life. I walked toward her cautiously.

"They told me I was never going to see you again," I said.

She smiled and slowly shook her head. "No, Dawn, that's not true."

Tears of relief rolled down my cheeks as I dropped to my knees and collapsed in her lap. The touch of her body made me feel as if I had safely arrived home from a terrifying battle.

Anne placed her arm inside the back of my jacket and lightly pressed down on my last three vertebrae. The pressure on my spine released a wave of warm energy that rolled up my back, through the top of my head, and back down the front of my body. My chest flooded with an all-encompassing sense of wholeness and peace.

"Get off of her!" the older woman said in a strong southern accent. She grabbed me by the jacket, yanked me off of Anne and threw me against the door. "Get out of here!"

My body felt like a shell, as if the woman had just torn me from the pulse of my own heart.

The woman pointed at me and laughed. "She's been a fool over you!" she said to Anne. "She's sick, dependent, enmeshed, obsessed!"

I stood paralyzed in the doorway.

"You were her therapist," the woman told Anne. "And you have no business in her life. I don't want you to see her again, ever!" She grabbed Anne by the hand and took her up a staircase, ridiculing me as she walked, convincing Anne to stay away. I watched in humility, longing for Anne to turn around, desperate to be back in the safety of her arms.

"Get out of here!" the woman yelled again. I turned away, feeling so repulsive, so worthless, that I never wanted to be seen again.

I ran out into the night, down a dark, narrow path when I heard a child cry. Another cry and I awoke. The sound was coming from my daughter Katie.

I jumped out of bed and ran to her room. But by the time I reached her, she had fallen back to sleep. I stumbled into the bathroom, got a drink of water, splashed a little on my face, then went back to bed. I lay there for the next hour staring at the ceiling praying. *Please help me, God. Please. What do I do now?*

In the morning, I awoke to a chanting in my mind, a gentle rhythm that sounded like background music in an elevator. I focused on the chanting until I could distinguish the words.

Love her with all your heart, with all your mind, and with all your soul. Love her with all your heart, with all your mind, and with all your soul. Love her with all your heart, with all your mind, and with all your soul.

I repeated the message out loud and burst into tears, finally receiving permission to do what my heart had long desired.

෴

I walked into my next therapy session and quickly shut the door, feeling anger shooting out of my eyes as I told Judith about the dream and the message I received that morning.

"In all the time that Anne's been gone," I said, "I have tried to find understanding through friends, therapists, and support groups. And never, not once, has anybody ever said to me, 'Why don't you just love her?'"

Judith was speechless.

"It's so damn simple."

She nodded. "I'm sorry, Dawn, and you have all the right in the world to be angry."

Neither one of us spoke for several minutes.

"Can you tell me more about the woman in your dream? The one who pulled you off of Anne."

"She was a bitch. A bitter, abrasive, condescending bitch."

"And who in your life do you think she represents?"

"I don't know. She laughed at me like my mother, but the ridicule felt like it was coming from society--the popular belief, or the latest therapeutic theory."

"And do I represent that to you?" she asked.

"Sometimes."

She winced and took a deep breath. "Close your eyes," she said.

"You're really pushing it."

"I know, but please do it anyway."

Why I obeyed her was beyond me. I closed my eyes and sat back in my chair.

"Bring back into your awareness the scene from the dream where the woman pulled you off Anne. When you have her in your mind, I want you to become her. Take on her consciousness."

As I centered my mind on the image of the woman, a subtle pain began to fill my chest. I was surprised at the tenderness behind her veneer.

"She's a very hurt person," I said. "She's been judged harshly and rejected and from her pain she does the same." The energy in my chest continued to swell, coming from my center, as if I had just connected through an umbilical cord to a large pool of worldwide suffering.

"This pain I feel, it's so deep... so vast... it goes beyond me. It feels like it is coming from the center of the earth." The anguish felt as though it was inflating my body. My voice rose as the words rolled off my tongue. "We don't understand who we are. When we judge ourselves, and when we judge others, we are tearing our soul apart." The pain was global, a universal heart being ignorantly destroyed by the individual cells of its own organism. My back arched from the energy, and my chest felt as though it was about to burst.

"Dawn, bring in somebody to help you. There's too much energy here. Ask what you need to do with it."

The Light and the woman in the shawl appeared. *Write about it.*

"I'm to write about it. We must stop hurting ourselves. We all live in one body and the judgments are destroying us. They are tearing apart the heart of the human organism."

The painful energy began to subside as I opened my eyes and caught my breath. "That was wild," I said as I shook my head.

"You're tapping into collective consciousness. That can be very powerful."

"It is excruciating. It's the same feeling I had in the dream when I was pulled from Anne. Like I had just been torn away from my own heart. But what I just experienced was much deeper. It's like our entire world feels this pain and, somehow, we don't know it. It's beneath the surface."

Judith leaned forward and nodded. We sat in stillness for a long moment. My chest still hurting from the experience.

"What did Anne represent to you in the dream?"

"My heart. My soul. She was kind and compassionate and I felt so loved and accepted by her. There was something I saw in her that was me. I can't explain it, but it was more than a projection. It was something very real."

"Projections are real."

"Yes, but it wasn't just in my mind. It was also in hers."

Judith's face was expressionless.

"I want you to go home and write more about the dream. Go into Anne's consciousness, the other woman's, and then back into yours. Write it like a play and describe each character. They all represent a part of you, and we want to try and understand them."

Her words went through me. "Judith, I'm supposed to love Anne with all my heart, all my mind and all my soul. That's a lot of energy to put into somebody who might not care if I still exist."

"Dawn, it doesn't matter how Anne feels. This is about you."

"It matters a lot to me how Anne feels," I said. "I want to believe that I connected to something other than myself."

"I think you have."

I looked at the floor and shook my head.

"Have you checked in to see where you are in the well?"

I closed my eyes and brought up the image. "It looks like I'm about half-way down the shaft."

"Good. The well represents your feelings of shame and how deep they are. You are making good progress becoming aware of them and releasing them from your body. Keep going to Tai Chi class. I think it's helping."

"What happens when I get to the bottom of the well?"

"I'm not sure, but I think we are going to find out soon."

Two weeks after Jeff left, Laura came over and stayed with the kids so I could fly to the wedding in Idaho. I boarded the flight with more anxiety than I usually had while flying. The thought of dropping to the bottom of the well, made every-day life feel more precarious.

When I landed, I took a cab to the hotel, a renovated hunting lodge that sat at the end of the lake, nestled in tall pines. I checked into our hotel and walked down to the shore. The late fall air was like a splash of cool water, the sky so blue it looked animated.

I spotted Jeff sitting on the dock, a fishing pole in one hand and a beer in the other. Maxx was lying next to him. I picked up a rock and lobbed it by his line. Jeff looked for the fish. Maxx raced toward me.

"Hi, boy," I said as he jumped to my chest.

Jeff reeled in his line and got up to hug me. "Get out of there, Maxx, she's my chick."

I wrapped my arms around him. His body felt hard, his eyes lonely.

"Did you miss me?" I asked.

"I think about you all the time," he replied as he kissed me.

He pulled me closer to his body and let out a sigh. "I have to be on time to this wedding," he said, "but can we please come back to this tonight?"

He pushed deeper into me. At that point, it wasn't something I wanted for myself. But I wanted him to know that I still loved him.

"I promise," I said as I ran my hand through his hair.

The wedding was held in an old, refurbished barn on the outskirts of town. The walls of the barn were paneled with pinewood and the floor-to-ceiling back doors had been converted to a pane-glass window that looked over a wheat field and into a meadow. We were seated when we arrived, and shortly after the bride and groom exchanged vows. Jeff squeezed my hand and then jumped up to help a group of guys convert the room into a dance hall.

The event looked like a high school reunion, and I was feeling apprehensive about seeing old friends. Word had gotten around that I had been sexually abused as a child and most of our friends knew my parents. A sense of dread tightened my gut as I walked toward the bathrooms and bumped into Jane, the groom's mother. Jane was a retired professor of medical genetics, a handsome gray-haired woman with the sturdy body of a mountain hiker and the soft lines of a woman aging gracefully. Her blue-water eyes lit up as she recognized me and something about her made me suddenly feel at ease.

"Motherhood must be agreeing with you," she said. "You look very different." She stared at me for several moments while other friends passed us in the hall, one woman from high school stopping for a brief chat. When the conversation hit a lull, Jane wove her arm around mine and walked me around the corner.

"Tell me what's happening to you," she said.

"What do you mean?"

"You look different. Your eyes have more clarity." I wasn't sure if she was sensing the change in my energy, or commenting on the eye contact we were having -- something I had always avoided with adults when I was a teenager. Feeling increasingly more comfortable with her, I explained that I had been releasing some old emotions. Her eyes continued to sparkle so I went a little further and told her about the therapy I had been doing and the images I had received. She smiled widely.

"You're having an awakening," she said. "I retired fifteen years ago, and I've been studying the process of transformation ever since. It's the most exciting thing I've ever done."

"It's exciting, all right."

"Dawn, this is the most wonderful time to be alive. The spiritual elements being discovered in physics, astronomy, psychology, and neurobiology are fascinating." She elaborated on a theory in physics. Seeing it was over my head, she slowed down and went back to common ground.

"Did your awakening begin spontaneously or did something trigger it?" she asked.

"I don't know. I just woke up one morning with a ball of energy hovering in the center of my chest, and then all hell broke loose."

Jeff came up and joined the conversation while Jane grabbed a pen from her purse and wrote down her phone number and address.

"I would love to talk to you more about this. I have built a wonderful home not far from you in Santa Barbara. It would be great fun if you could come visit sometime."

I thanked her for the invitation and went into the party. Jeff and I stood at the bar while friends approached. To my surprise, the encounters were not awkward; whether in a warm embrace or words of condolences, everybody who knew shared their sympathy and similar sentiments. "You were always so driven. We knew you were running from something. We just didn't know what." I appreciated their insights. I had always realized I was driven, but I had no idea at the time that I was running.

The champagne began to pour and for the next eight hours we sang, danced, and laughed over old stories while Jeff participated in a few drinking games along the way. At midnight, I lifted the car keys from his back pocket.

"I can drive," he said in a slurred voice.

"I'm sure you can, but I need the practice."

I rounded up Maxx and put him in the van while Jeff staggered into the front seat and hung his head out the window. The map was on the floor, and I picked it up as we left the parking lot. Five miles later we were lost. I pulled over and turned on the light. It was forty degrees and I was freezing, but Jeff had passed out against the door, and I didn't dare close the window. The only thing worse than throwing up myself was watching somebody else do it.

Maxx came up from the back and licked my face. Even he smelt like beer. I pushed him away. "Go sit down, boy."

I looked at the directions again. Turn left at the tree stump, right at the end of the Murphy's green barn. It was pitch black out. How was I supposed to find a tree stump? I rolled up the map and hit Jeff over the head.

"Will you get up?" I yelled.

He didn't move.

For the next hour I was lost, driving down dark rural streets in Idaho, my lips turning blue from the cold as Jeff snored.

"Why do you do this?" I screamed. "Why do I do this?" I said under my breath.

I finally found a main street and followed a truck into town and pulled into the hotel parking lot exhausted. Jeff didn't budge. I threw a blanket over him and locked the car, figuring he had too much alcohol in him to freeze to death.

I rolled over in the morning. Sometime during the night, Jeff had made it to our room and was sleeping in his clothes next to me. I laid there repulsed by the smell of his breath. Since we were in high school, I always felt that his drinking somehow compensated for inadequacy in me. But, I was starting to realize that was part of my shame and I deserved more than his bouts of black-out inebriation.

I crawled out of bed. "I'm getting too old for this," I said.

"What? Just because you had to drive me home."

I wasn't in the mood for an argument and my flight home was in a few hours. I went into the bathroom to pack, neither one of us speaking until after breakfast. He drove me to the airport without words and gave me a quick kiss goodbye at the curb. I closed the door to the van not feeling much of anything.

During the flight home, I closed my eyes and checked in with my inner world. The platform I was on had sunken to a lower level and at the top of the shaft was the image of the woman in the orange shawl.

Pay attention. Stay aware.

I felt a subtle dread in the pit of my stomach. I had descended further from the light. The well was getting darker and the damp, cold chill that ran through my body gave me the sense that I was going through a spiritual hazing and the obstacles were about to get harder.

On Friday, I took the kids to school and went to Tai Chi. We started with our arms stretched out to our sides, our palms open as if we were trying to hold open closing doors in an elevator. I pushed out as far as I could until I felt a deep strain run up my arms. The seconds now went by like minutes as we held the pose.

"Do you still like this?" Laura whispered as her hands and knees began to tremble.

"No. But it helps," I said as we moved to the next position, our arms bent in front of us as if we were squeezing down on a large beach ball. I closed my eyes and began to notice a rising anxiety. With it came the image of my childhood home. A cloud of white smoke was bellowing from the front door as if it was calling me to enter.

The following day, my mother came up for her monthly visit with the kids. I usually left an hour before she arrived and returned only after I knew she was gone, but Isabella was out that day, so for the first time in eight months, I was going to see my mother.

I struggled through the morning picking up clothes and putting away dishes, fueling my anger with every breath. How could I stay civil? She'd betrayed me as child, as an adult, as a human being, and now with the full knowledge of the abuse in my childhood, I would have to face her again.

At eleven o'clock, the bell rang and Jen ran to open the door. My mother walked in wearing a bright orange pant-suit and matching orange lipstick that accented the smile that wrapped around her face. She was carrying a batch of chocolate chip cookies and a bouquet of yellow fresh cut flowers.

"It's so good to see you, Baby," she said as she put down her gifts and threw her arms around me.

I felt like I'd just landed in the twilight zone.

"You look good, Honey. Are you feeling better?" she asked.

"I'm working on it."

"I think about you all the time, and I hope you know I love you."

Who was this lady? "The kids are upstairs," I said. "I have some errands to run."

"Take all the time you need." She unloaded a bag of presents while I walked slowly out of the house.

Didn't I hate her? Maybe not. Maybe I'd forgotten about the good things, the parts of her I loved. She was warm, attractive, and generous. She loved and nurtured my children. And she genuinely seemed to care about me. Was this the same mother I'd spoken to on the phone? The woman who would rather believe an Oprah show than me?

I couldn't remember what I was shopping for, so I drove to Laura's house, borrowed a room, and took a nap. Three hours later I woke up just as confused, just as tired.

I pulled up in the driveway and all the kids were playing ball in the street, their faces smeared with chocolate.

Mom came up and kissed me good-bye. "Honey, if you ever need me, you know I'll be there."

I stared at her as she got in her car. *What? I did need you. You weren't there. You're cold, ignorant, and defensive! Why are you acting like you're not?*

When she left, I put Matthew and Katie down for a nap and then checked on Jen in the playroom. She was sitting at the craft table spilling out the contents of a gift bag my mother had given her, sorting the candy from the crayons and stickers.

"What's this?" I asked as I picked up an old photo of me out of the bag.

"It's a picture. Grandma wanted to show me how much I looked like you when you were a kid."

I nodded. I was about Jen's age in the photo standing on my red scooter in front of my childhood home. The look of suspicion on my face was palpable.

"What else did she say?"

"Nothing. Just that she loves that picture of you."

Jen put the crayons in the bag while I stared at the photo. The house where I grew up felt like it was again beckoning me to enter. I cleared my throat.

"Can I watch *Little Mermaid*?" she asked.

"Sure, Honey. I'll turn it on"

🐚

I went into my next session with Judith and told her about my encounter with my mother and the mixed emotions I was having about it. She listened, then unwrapped a small piece of hard candy and put it in her mouth.

"Dawn, I'm sure your mother is a compassionate woman who loves you and your children deeply. And she can also be cold, narrow-minded and defensive. It's not a black-and-white world. Both sides of your mother exist."

"Then why am I so confused?"

"Because as a child you tried to make sense of the world by seeing it in terms of black and white, all or nothing, good and evil. But both good and bad traits exist in people. It's the same principle we discussed in regard to your father."

"But her words are so different from her actions, they seem to be coming from two different value systems."

"Because they do. People have different values for different situations. Your mother's compassion in one situation is as real as her defensiveness and denial in another. Both traits exist, and you need to keep telling yourself that."

"But she doesn't see me. She's denying what happened to me and the suffering it has caused me and my family."

"Your mother is denying her own pain, and as long as she does, there is no way she can see all the parts of you."

I handed Judith the picture of me on my red scooter. "She gave Jen this."

Judith looked at the picture and handed it back to me. "What do you see in it?"

"Mostly my childhood home in the background. The door is closed, there are no windows in the front of the house. It feels like it's a prison in my mind. And, some part of me lives in there."

I dropped my head into my hands and closed my eyes. When I did, I saw myself drop to the bottom of the well.

"I have to go into that house," I said. "Something keeps telling me I have to go back there."

"Why?"

"I'm not sure. But right now, I'm stuck in a well of shame, and it feels like if I want to get out, I'm going to have to go into that house."

"You want to do a guided imagery?"

"No. But I don't have a choice. That house is in my way."

"Dawn, you always have a choice."

"And I choose not to live in fear anymore. Whatever happened, it happened in the past."

Judith nodded. "Okay, but I'm not letting you go back into the house as a child. I want you to remain an adult. Is there an image you have of a safe place? A place where you can go if the house becomes overwhelming?" I told her about the image of the small garden with the manicured lawn that I imagined when I was working with Anne.

"Great. Let's start there."

I closed my eyes, took a few deep breaths, and began to imagine the garden.

The grounds now appeared spacious and light and the tall bushes and dark forest that once enclosed the yard were gone. Beyond the garden there was now a valley of yellow wheat grass and rolling, green hills.

"When you get to the garden, I want you to call up any children that are still with you." The five-year-old appeared, her face looking more like a child, trusting, tender and innocent. "Ask her who she wants to stay with her while you go back into your childhood home."

Anne.

I brought in an image of Anne, a scene that came alive with vivid color as Anne knelt and opened her arms and the child ran into her warm embrace.

"When the five-year-old is safe," Judith said, "leave the garden and go to the entrance of the home in the picture." I imagined myself leaving the garden and standing in front of the beige double door. I took a deep breath and opened it slowly.

The house was dark and stuffy, the windows looked like they had been closed for decades. I walked past the musty avocado-green couches, opening the window curtains to air out the room.

"Where are you?" Judith asked.

"I'm in the living room, looking down the hall. It's dark and narrow. I'm starting to feel the terror."

"Take a few deep breaths and take something with you. You don't have to go down that hall by yourself."

In the image a large, wood baseball bat appeared in my hands. I slowly walked down the hall and turned into the bathroom, flipped on the light and noticed the shower curtain was closed. I clutched my bat and flung open the plastic.

"Oh, God," I moaned as I looked at the bathtub where my father took me after the rape.

"What's happening?" Judith asked.

"There's a red bloodstained ring around the tub. It's my blood. I have to get it off." I started to pant as I rushed to the cabinet under the sink to look for some cleanser. I swung open the doors, and a hand, severed at the wrist, rolled out of the cabinet. I started to cry.

"Judith, my hand, my writing hand, it's under the sink."

"Do you need to put the hand back on?" she asked.

"Yes." I picked up the hand and slipped it on mine like a translucent glove. A warm sensation radiated from my palm up my arm and into my heart, as if I have reconnected my own natural gift. My form of expression severed by the childhood assault.

I grabbed the bat, left the bathroom, and went down the hall to my parents' room. I opened the door and saw the ghost of my father chained naked to his bed. Hovering around him were the three friends of his that molested me.

He laughed at me. "It's only a game," he said.

I jumped on his bed and started to strangle him. "I don't have to do this anymore. I never ever have to do this again."

Then I picked up my bat and swung at the men hitting them until they disintegrated.

I told Judith what I was doing.

"What about your father?"

I felt a pain in my chest and tears ran down my cheeks. "I... I... I can't remove him. He hurt me, but he is the only one protecting the house." My head hurt from a childlike confusion.

"Okay," Judith said, "then leave him chained to the bed and keep moving through the house." I left my parents room and walked down the hall to my bedroom. I turned the knob slowly and pushed open the door. In front of me, standing against the window, was a ghost image of my mother. Her stare was empty. The floor was covered with coffee mugs half full of wine. I picked up the mugs and started smashing them against the wall.

"I hate this!" I yelled. "I hate this!"

Judith asked me what was happening, and before I could answer a brilliant, white light from outside the window disintegrated the wall and sucked out my mother. My body convulsed. My chest felt as though it had been torn open by a knife.

"She's dead!" I cried out to Judith. "The abuse killed my mom!"

"Keep breathing," Judith said.

"She couldn't help me," I cried as my body began to tremble. "She wasn't strong enough... oh, God, it wasn't her fault... she wasn't strong enough."

"Keep breathing, Dawn. The shaking can't hurt you, but you have to keep breathing."

"My mom's dead! The Light took her! Judith, I can't stand this pain. My chest feels like it's bleeding."

"Ask the Light if it can help take the edge off."

My attention was drawn to the top corner of the room. Hovering there, like an angel of light, was the image of Anne.

I doubled over in tears.

"Anne's here. She's always been here." I tried to catch my breath. "I've been so ashamed of my feelings for her, but this relationship kept me alive. It kept me alive."

Judith's voice was somber. "You don't have to be ashamed of your love for Anne. She reflected the light in you, and that light has always been with you."

Judith loaded my hand with tissue. "What do you need to do next?"

I looked around. My childhood home was disintegrated by the Light. The darkness was gone and an image of me sitting in the bottom of the well appeared. A thought that felt like a command entered my mind.

Release yourself.

A staircase formed from a wall in the well. With a sense of budding elation, I climbed to the top and opened my eyes.

CHAPTER TWELVE

"The dad's home," yelled Jeff from the entry. He clomped up the stairs as the kids screamed, jumping to get out of the tub where I was bathing them. Matthew and Katie barely toweled off then ran naked half-covered with bubbles into Jeff's arms. Jen raced to put on one of his T-shirts and then jumped on him from behind. Jeff carried the kids to the couch in the playroom. He had grown a short beard. The deep lines on his forehead were gone and his skin was tanned from the sun.

"How is everybody doing?" he asked as he reached over and gave me a hug.

"We're doing okay," I said as I kissed him.

"Did you bring home any dead fish?" Matthew asked.

"No but I brought you home some presents."

The kids ran circles around the room as Jeff pulled a few toys out of his backpack. They picked between stuffed animals of fish and games that had fish on them. We played the games until it was time for bed, then Jeff tucked them in, telling them stories with no apparent end until one by one they fell asleep.

He came into our room afterward and unpacked his clothes. For the next hour he told me a series of stories about his travels. The friends and relatives he connected with and the various bodies of water in the western states where he fished. There were stories, inside of stories, and the fish got bigger every time. But I listened, intently, until finally there was a suitable pause.

"Did you have any revelations about us?" I asked as he got into bed.

"Actually, I did. I think that maybe God wanted us to be together so I could help you through this part of your life. And maybe when your healing process is over, you won't need me anymore."

I stared at him in disbelief. Unable to find the words to answer.

"But, I don't know what I would do without you," he said, "so I made a decision."

"What's that?"

"I decided to stop drinking. I don't know if it will help but I'm willing to give it a try."

A smile wrapped around my face as a sense of safety filled my chest.

"Thank you," I said, "I don't know what I would do without you either."

That week Jeff volunteered at the elementary school. He convinced a few other parents to pitch in and together they began to build a schoolyard garden. When he wasn't at the school he was playing with the kids or fishing down at the beach. He seemed happier than I had seen him in years, with little concern about working again. As usual, I wasn't so carefree. The money we received from the sale of the company would only last a few years and I was hoping we could put much of it away for a college fund for the kids. But, I wasn't ready to find work again either. And I still had no vision of what my future would look like.

On Thursday, I went to see Judith. It had been over a week since I released myself from the feelings that were represented in the well, yet I still felt polluted by the toxicity of shame. I sat down in her office and pulled a bottle of water out of my bag trying to drench the feelings of filth still lingering in my body.

"You look more peaceful," she said as she pulled off her reading glasses and sat down in her chair.

"I do feel less burdened. But my body aches. And, I have a strange craving, like I am chemically addicted to the well and I want to crawl back into it."

"You've been in that well most of your life. It's natural that you would feel pulled to go back to the only place you've ever known."

"But I feel toxic, like the well's heavy, polluted smell is still clinging to me."

She nodded. "If you took an object from a well where it had been for thirty years, the object would still have the smell and the energy of the well."

"Then how do I cleanse myself?"

"Close your eyes."

I looked at her. "You don't believe in much foreplay, do you?"

"I thought we did have foreplay."

"I guess it's all in the perception."

She chuckled and told me to take a few deep breaths. When I did, she asked me to go to the well. On my third breath, I saw the image of me sitting on a patch of green grass next to a deep hole in the ground. My body yearning to jump in.

"I want you to ask somebody to come in and give you some guidance." The image of the woman in the orange shawl appeared along with the brilliant dense Light that was slightly larger than a human body.

Do not return to the well.

An iron grate slammed down over the hole. Through a telepathic thought, the woman told me to follow her. She led me down a path that began several yards from the well. The heavy vegetation of a tropical forest began to appear as we walked through a warm, light-gray mist held in by the tall fan palms that filtered in long streams of soft, white light. After a few moments, we came to a natural pool of water. A clear waterfall that cascaded like melted glass over a six-foot ledge fed the pool. At the other end of the pond were small rock streams that drained the pool into a creek below it. I bent down and touched the water; it felt like tepid, liquid silk and left a light, gold sheen on my hands.

"Dawn, what's happening?" Judith asked.

"She is showing me a pool to cleanse in."

"Good. Bring in whatever you'll need to be comfortable." I imagined myself naked in a big, white, cotton robe and then brought in the image of my blue, high-back beach chair to place next to the stream as I went in and out of the pool.

"Is there anything else you need to know, or take with you, before we wrap up?"

The image of the Light was suddenly by my side. *Write the book.*

I repeated the message to Judith.

"Okay, thank the woman and the Light, and when you are ready open your eyes and bring your consciousness back into the room."

I opened my eyes and looked at Judith. "That was interesting," I said "What do you make of it?"

"I think you're in the process of mourning the process. There is a very real loss involved when we transform out of old familiar ways of being in the world, and it takes discipline to not return to negative thought patterns."

"You mean I could end up back in the well?"

"I don't actually think you could go fully back to where you have been. The images and the messages you are receiving are empowering and healing you. But to stay out of the well, you will have to choose not to go there."

"How do I do that?"

"Choose your thoughts and actions based on what will strengthen your spirit, not your fears and insecurities. And right now, your spirit, and a rather powerful universal one, wants you to write."

I looked down and started rubbing my right hand. "I meant to ask you about that. The hand I retrieved, my writing hand. It must have been severed in the abuse."

"I think it was. Child abuse can detach us from our nature and our natural gifts. It keeps children stuck in small dark wells where the shame they feel keeps them from fully blossoming and expressing their gifts. And, sadly, it robs the world of their contribution.

"So, if this didn't happen to me, I would have become a writer?"

"You are a writer. You are just retrieving that part of yourself."

"But what does the Light want me to write a book about?"

"Write about what's happening to you. The Light is a universal figure, and it is leading you somewhere for some reason and it clearly wants you to write about it. I believe that is the calling."

Her words struck me like a neon sign. I felt like I had finally been hit by the obvious.

I went home for lunch but couldn't eat, my body still felt like I had inhaled the fumes from an oil refinery. I took a couple aspirin, went up to the nest, and lay down on the bed until the well appeared. When it did, I walked back to the pool and took off my robe. The tall vegetation that shaded the pool gave me a sense of protection. I stepped into the water and waded under the falls, the warm liquid caressing my hair, washing my face and massaging my neck and shoulders. It felt as though a refreshing peace was pouring through my body, as though...

"Mom, we're home!" Matthew screamed through the doorway. The image disappeared.

"Can I have something to eat?" Katie yelled right behind him.

The mother from the carpool came up to the door. "Are you home?"

"Yes, I'm here. Thanks for picking them up," I said.

I jumped up to go downstairs, feeling lighter, cleaner, and hungry.

I began writing the book that night. When I recalled the journey I had been on for the past few years, words poured through my fingers like a dam had broken. Conversations in therapy were stored in my mind as if I had a tape recorder in my head. I could remember every word, scent and nuance as if it happened yesterday. And with every page I wrote, the depression was lifting.

For the next several months, I volunteered with Jeff at the elementary school during the day, and in the early mornings I would get up and write. Maxx would rest at my feet while the words continued to flow much like the journey did. And as lingering emotions seeped up, I would go back to the image of the pool and imagine myself being cleansed in the shimmering water. That became the routine until late April, when the story I was writing, caught up to the one I was living, and I still didn't have an ending.

To give me some quiet time to work on the book, Jeff offered to take the kids to Sea World while I drove up to Santa Barbara for the weekend. It was early May when I checked into the small Spanish-style bed and breakfast. It felt good to be away, and to be alone for a few days.

I spent the first day walking the town feeling more alive and alert than I had in years. The sidewalks were lined with tall palm trees and white stucco buildings partially covered by bright pink bougainvillea vines that grew toward the sun. I meandered through the small bookstores and gift shops before landing in a patio café for a salad peppered with fresh seafood. At sunset, I walked back to my room, took a long bath and went to bed early.

In the morning, I woke to the sound of a spring rain shower trickling down the red tiled roof. Relieved that I didn't have to get up to tend to anybody, I pulled the white bed comforter up to my chin and closed my eyes again. A moment later, the Light appeared. It looked to be twice my size, hovering like a brilliant star just a few yards above me.

Before I could open my eyes, it became active. Green, white, and blue light rays shot out from the Light and into my body. My eyes flew open, and I jerked up in bed.

"What do you want from me?"

Suddenly, a vibration of energy like a snake uncoiling moved up my spine. My body, doing something without my permission, left me feeling completely out of control. I jumped out of bed and paced the floor wishing I was home. Wishing there was at least somebody else in the room.

I grabbed a pillow off the bed and held it to my chest. The base of my spine again began to vibrate, and suddenly powerful sexual sensations flushed through my body taking me in seconds to the brink of orgasm. Then, just as quickly, I dropped into terror, an extreme survival fear that lasted for minutes. I knew from what Russ had taught me that the Charka's in those areas were rapidly opening and as the energy moved through my body, I felt a warm expanding sensation in my heart all the way up to the crown of my head. Moments later, I stared out the window as my eyes clouded with a vision, an image of me reaching out to touch translucent figures of strangers who I realized were an extension of me, all of us part of a greater organism. An all-encompassing feeling of love filled my body as I realized every human being was immensely precious and a part of me. Just as I was a part of them. The awareness then faded and my hands began to shake.

I rifled through the hotel mini-bar and opened a granola bar. My hands still shaking as I raised it to my mouth. I thought for a moment then reached for my purse. Jane, the groom's mother, said she lived in Santa Barbara. If anybody knew what was happening to me, she would. I found her number. My fingers trembling as I called her. On the third ring she picked up. I told her about the experience of the Light and the sensations I was feeling in my body. She invited me to come right over.

I pulled into her driveway. Jane came out from behind her cottage style home in a dark blue rain jacket. Her gracefully aging body felt sturdy and strong as I hugged her hello.

"Did you have any problems finding the house?"

"No, and I'm very glad I'm here." As we walked into the kitchen, I told her about the image of the Light and the flow of energy that was barreling through my body, recounting the sensations without taking a breath.

"Whatever is happening to me is happening too fast," I said. "I can't control it--it's taking me over."

She poured me a hot cup of tea and stepped up to her library, where she pulled several books from her shelf and laid them on the table.

"What you're experiencing," she said, "is really quite normal for the process you're in."

"This is normal?"

She nodded. "In the base of the spine there is a coil of energy that is known in many cultures as the Kundalini.

When it is activated, the Kundalini energy moves through the chakras system. The sensations you felt--of losing control, intense sexual arousal and visions of our connectedness to one another--are reactions to the energy as it opens the root, heart, and crown chakras." Her voice deepened. "The Kundalini is powerful. If it moves through your body too quickly, it can be very damaging."

I pushed away my tea. My fingers still trembling.

"Dawn, I've been worried about you. It's not advisable to do this type of deep spiritual work without a teacher who has had firsthand experience with the process of transformation."

"I have a good therapist."

"Has she done this kind of work before?"

"No, but she's probably read about it." I stood up and started to pace. "Jane, I need to slow this energy down. It's too much."

She got up and went to the refrigerator. "Sit down, I'll make you a steak."

"A steak?"

"You need a heavy meal, something that will ground you for a couple of hours."

I wasn't hungry, but I forced myself to eat. After a couple of bites my mind and body began to slow down.

"Jane, if the image I received really is the Light of God, why didn't I feel loved when it appeared?"

"I believe the love comes when you open up and actually accept the Light. The blue and green light you describe probably activated the Kundalini energy. It's preparing you for the divine encounter."

"What happens in the divine encounter?"

"Typically, people see a face of God. And they undeniably know that this intelligence exists. But based on what you have told me about the road you have been on, it sounds like you are receiving some kind of a message. Quite possibly a prophecy."

"What kind of prophecy?"

"I don't know. You will have to have the encounter to find out."

I took a deep breath, and another bite of my steak, hoping it would all just go away.

"When you get home, you can read some of the books I will give you. Most of them describe the roller-coaster sensations of the Kundalini energy as part of the spiritual transformation process, a phase that is often referred to as the *dark night of the soul*. It's the most rapid and turbulent part of the cleansing process."

"My mind feels like it's being annihilated."

"In a sense, it is, and your reaction is typical. People often want to quit at this point. But you don't want to get stuck in the Kundalini energy phase, it amplifies your longings, insecurities and fears. For the sake of your own comfort, you need to keep going."

I spent the rest of the day in my hotel room reading the books she gave me. Christian, Buddhist, and mystical Jewish and Hindu literature that depicted the stages of emotional and spiritual evolution. The onset of depression, high anxiety, heightened intuition or internal messages were all a part of the process. As was the dark night of soul, the awareness that we are not separate from one another, a deep yearning for a loved one, and an encounter with the divine.

I could see that I had traveled through most of the stages and the context behind the awakening process brought me some peace of mind. Yet at the same time, the yearnings were intensifying and the ache to be back in Anne's arms, to finally feel safe again, was so strong I couldn't sleep. I couldn't even look at her picture.

In the morning, I met Jane in town and we went for a walk before I left for home. She cautioned me to take it slowly. "Ground yourself with heavy foods, routines, and people who make you feel secure."

"How much longer is this going to last?"

"You are almost there. But be careful. You are being prepared to receive something from what we refer to as God. Those levels of consciousness can be very hard on your body."

My stomach tensed. "This process kind of sucks," I said as I hugged her goodbye.

She chuckled. "Yes, it certainly can feel that way."

On Tuesday, I started my session with Judith telling her about my trip and my experience with the Kundalini energy. As I assumed, Judith hadn't experienced it, but she had read about it and the effects it has had on people throughout history.

"Dawn, I think I need some clarity," she said. "It's natural for the expansion of your consciousness to cause some paranoia, but it sounds like you're afraid of the Light."

"I am."

"Why? Most people would love that experience."

My hands started to sweat. "What if the Light tells me something I don't want to hear? What if it makes me do something I don't want to do? What if it brainwashes me? Sends me out to parties to tell people Jesus loves them? I don't want to be like that. I don't even like those people."

"You have some interesting associations. Do you have a Christian upbringing?"

"No. But I have felt judged by people who act like they are better than me because they follow Jesus. It's annoying."

"That is annoying. But again, that has more to do with them than you."

I felt my stomach twist and my feet turn inward.

"The Light has so much power. What if it tries to hurt me?"

Judith winced. "Dawn the Light is not your human father. It's here to help you. I think you can trust it."

I looked up at the ceiling, trying to stop my tears.

"Have you had other clients experience the Light?"

"Yes, but the image you described is both universal and subjective. Based on people's cultures and experiences, the Light has been interpreted as being God, Jesus, the Buddha, Mohammed. There have been many different names for the same experience."

"What happens when people experience it?"

"They don't need to see me anymore."

It was the first time the thought of leaving therapy had entered my mind.

"But, Dawn, I feel compelled to warn you. I believe what you are going through is a transformation that seems to be exposing you to the awareness of a higher self. But, I agree with Jane, there also seems to be a universal element to your process. If you are indeed receiving direct communication from a spiritual dimension to bring to others, it could be difficult for your mind and body to absorb that kind of energy in human form. Historically, people who have had those kinds of encounters have had a difficult time assimilating it."

I stared at her but didn't respond. I felt like I was the cowardly lion about to enter the great cathedral of Oz.

I stood up to leave.

"I'm here anytime you need me. You have my home phone number. Just call me. We are going to get you through this."

It was the middle of May, and for the next week I felt as though my body chemistry was again changing. I could tolerate only fruits and vegetables. My thirst increased and I craved lemon water. I knew I was going through another type of cleansing--and it felt like the final rinse. I calmed myself by looking at Anne's picture. If God was as gentle as she was, I had nothing to fear.

I woke up one morning and pulled out her photo. My capacity to love her was still growing and I was realizing things about her that I hadn't realized before. Just a few months ago, I'd thought if she loved me, she would have stayed in contact. Now I was starting to believe that she didn't stay in contact because she loved me. Jen walked in and jumped in my bed.

"What are you looking at?" she asked.

I showed her the picture of Anne holding a rabbit. "Do you see God in this picture?"

"Yeah," she said. "It's the rabbit."

I looked at the photo. The rabbit did look more present than Anne.

"Why do you look at her picture?" Jen asked.

"I guess it reminds me of something I'm supposed to remember."

"What's that?"

"I don't know. When I remember it, I'll let you know."

She giggled and crawled under my arm as I pulled the blanket around her shoulders.

"Jen, what do you think God is?"

"I think it's an invisible power," she said.

"Have you ever seen God, besides in rabbits?"

"I see God everywhere."

I held her closer, giving her the security of a warm parent while I asked the questions of a frightened child.

"If God wanted to talk to you, would that scare you?" I asked.

She giggled. "It would surprise me, but it wouldn't scare me."

"What do you think God would want to say?"

"I think God just wants people to feel better."

"And how does He do that?"

"He breaks open their love box and gives them a newer, cleaner one. So people can hold more love."

I stared at the ceiling, wondering what well of knowledge she so easily tapped.

"Does it hurt to have your love box opened?"

"No. It's the best thing that could ever happen to you."

Friday morning Jeff and Matthew left for a weekend fishing trip. Matthew came in at 5:00 a.m. and kissed me goodbye. I rolled over and went back to sleep, and in my light slumber, I dreamt of pairs of large boa constrictors intertwined in a line blocking me as I tried to leave my home. There was a pair of snakes intertwined on my lawn, on my garage floor, and on the brick patio entrance to my house. The dreams weren't frightening, just unusual and vivid.

I awoke at seven and went in to take a shower. As the steam rose toward the ceiling, I noticed my body felt lighter, and my head felt as though it were expanding. As the day went on, I continued to get the sensation of being lifted, as if I were in a high-speed elevator being pulled away from gravity. At times it made me feel lightheaded, but I knew I wasn't sick, and I dreaded what was coming.

I left a message with Judith and tried to eat some lunch but could barely swallow down a few bites. For the rest of the day all I could tolerate was juice and water.

Judith called that evening. I told her how I was feeling and described the dreams about the snakes. "Do you think the snakes represented an abuse memory?"

"No. I don't think you're in individual consciousness anymore. Snakes intertwined is a symbol of man's interconnection with the Divine. The dream may be a foreshadowing to the levels of consciousness you are entering."

"I don't like this, Judith."

"I'm here this weekend if you need me. But I think the best thing to do is center yourself. You have been prepared for this. Check in with the Light and fasten your seat belt."

I fed the girls dinner and soon after tucked them into bed. Around ten o'clock I dosed off and was awakened at 3:00 a.m. by a full moon beaming through an arched window in my bedroom. I opened my eyes and sat up in bed. As I did, the top of my head felt as though it was being dilated—spreading open like the walls of a cervix in final labor. I closed my eyes to center myself. When I did, the woman and the Light appeared in the center of my mind, and I heard an inaudible command.

Get ready to write.

I turned on the light and grabbed my journal and a pen from the nightstand. When I closed my eyes again, I was standing next to the image of a vast hole on the floor of space that appeared to be the center of all creation. The image felt alive with a pulse, a perfect symmetrical circle with smooth edges that cascade up into space and time. It felt like I was at the epicenter of all of life's energy, at the base of a universal organism that brought forth all things. I sat up straight in bed. I instinctively knew I was in the presence of a divine source and the grandeur of the experience made me feel like I was the size of an ant at the foot of a king. I was humbled to my very core and instinctively bowed my head out of reverence.

I was then told to write. I touched my pen to the page and waited. A moment later, the dictation began. The information pulsing up through the center of creation in clear inaudible words that I wrote down as they were given to me.

The evolution of your species has begun. The dawn of a new consciousness is here. Don't be frightened this is a gentle process. You will receive everything you need to make your transformation safely. Watch for the signs. I have sent other messengers. They will appear soon. They will lead you through different stages as your species evolves. Sound your trumpets. A new beginning has arrived.

The discomfort began to subside as the crown of my head seemed to ease back to its natural state. I read the words to myself out loud, in complete awe of the experience, knowing that what I just wrote is nothing I would have personally thought or written. Sound your trumpets, a new beginning has arrived sounded like a clear announcement. The new consciousness rising felt like a positive change that will transition us into a gentler world and it was made clear to me that I was the first in a series of messengers. As I read it again, I was comforted by the words that we will receive everything we needed. That as divinely as I had been led, others would be led too.

I closed my journal and lay back in bed. For the next hour, I stared at the ceiling wishing the summons was over, but knowing it wasn't over yet. I sensed there was more to come, but as a human, I could only stay so long in such high levels of consciousness.

The next day was marked by the same sensations of being elevated. I couldn't eat much. I was lightheaded at times and the fatigue and bloated feelings continued. At times it felt like altitude sickness, as if I was adjusting to climbing to the top of a 14,000-foot mountain. By the afternoon, I noticed Jen had been caught up in the same sensations.

"I feel funny, Mom. Like something's happening to my head." Both the girls slept off and on most of the day, and that night after Katie went down, I tucked Jen into bed. As I kissed her goodnight, she turned to me with the most radiant smile.

"You look so happy," I said.

Her eyes twinkled like an angel. "Mom, God just opened my love box."

We were in the same level of consciousness, but I wasn't having the same experience. The anticipation of another night of messages had me feeling anxious and fatigued. After I tucked Jen in, I wrapped myself in one of Jeff's flannel shirts, drank a glass of water and calmed myself down by looking at Anne's picture. An hour later, I fell asleep.

At 4:00 a.m., I awoke to the same experience I'd had the morning before. The crown of my head opening like a cervix, then again, I heard the inaudible summons to write. I grabbed my journal and a pen and closed my eyes to center myself. In my mind's eye, the woman and the Light appeared, giving way to the grand opening, a vast active hole in space that appeared to be the center of all creation. I felt the humble and meager size of my presence then placed the tip of my pen to my journal. A moment later, the dictation began. The information emerging from the center of the vast crater. I wrote the words down as they were given to me.

This is a delicate time. You need to take care of each other. There are brothers and sisters among you who now embody my energy. Find them.

> *They know of the Light and they will have no*
> *prejudices. Let the people who know, lead. Trust*
> *them. They are me.*
>
> *It is very important to watch for the leaders*
> *because one is not real. He will have prejudices.*
> *Do not follow prejudice. It can only hurt you.*
> <u>*Do not follow prejudice*</u>*. It is not real, it is not*
> *me. There are people in your churches and*
> *synagogues who embody the Light--follow them.*

Do not follow prejudice was heavily emphasized, as if the telepathic words became louder and even more authoritative when those sentences were being communicated.

I was then told to clarify who I was as the writer of this message. I didn't know myself until the information entered my mind. In contrast to the universal messages, although I still felt aligned with God, the centered feeling in my body and the softer tone made me realize that the "I" in this message referred to me personally.

> *I am a messenger, not a healer. Others will come*
> *to help heal you. Do not follow me. I am not who*
> *you are looking for. I can only give direction. Go*
> *to your churches and synagogues for your healers.*
>
> *All will transform. Allow your circumstances*
> *to transform you as I have done. The more we*
> *volunteer to do this, the less suffering we will*
> *call upon ourselves.*

The expanded feeling at the top of my head began to subside. I wanted to ask a question about the churches and synagogues, but it was clear that it was one-way communication, and it was not mine to question. I laid down on my pillow and read the messages out loud. The sentence that it was a delicate time gave me trepidation, but I don't believe that was the sentiment of the message. It felt more like, as we begin this transition our species will become more sensitive and that kindness toward one another was necessary as we begin to evolve to a new level of consciousness.

I continued to read what had just been given to me. I had been exposed to enough Christianity to recognize the anti-Christ message, but I have never given it much credibility until that night. It felt very real and incredibly significant to avoid. It was profoundly clear that great destruction will come from following a prejudiced leader.

The following day was a quiet one. The girls and I went to the community pool in the morning then returned home to take naps and watch Disney movies. We all fell asleep early that night and just after 4:00 a.m. I was awakened by the same sensation, the crown of my head expanding. I sat up in bed, grabbed my journal, and once again found myself beside a vast and active opening, what felt to me to be the center of creation. But this time, when I closed my eyes, I was shown a vision.

In the vision, millions and millions of people were dying, souls rising from earth by some form of global annihilation. The terror that came with the scene was more intense than any fear I had known. As if I was standing above a dark earth watching most of the people, the families, the children, suffer and rapidly perish. I was so terrified I got up out of bed, grabbed a blanket, and curled up against the corner wall in my closet. The vision continued as the souls continued to rapidly ascend. The threat to our humanity was so immense that I was reduced to a trembling animal. A few minutes later, my terror subsided, and I was again summoned to write. The information coming from the center of creation. The inaudible dictation was loud and clear.

> *This is not necessary. Spare your brothers and sisters this suffering by learning to love now. Transform your individual consciousness by choice. There is time to prepare. There is time to breed the strong, the healthy. There is time to stop the apocalypse. There is time for a gentle change. Do not fear, liberation is near and there is time to do it peacefully.*

The discomfort in the crown of my head began to subside as I put down my pen and closed my journal. The experiences were finally over and a calmness emerged from within me. I slowly got up from the closet and went back to bed. I was so profoundly stunned by the divinity in the information, I could barely speak for days.

Judith called on Monday to see what happened over the weekend. But the experience was so powerful, so extraordinary, it was a week before the shock had subsided, and I was able to bring in the messages.

I sat down in my chair, told her what happened over those three nights, then handed her my journal.

"Wow," she said as she read. "These are powerful. How are you feeling?"

"I feel like a fish who was just pulled out of the pond and then sent back in to deliver a message from the pond keeper. My body still feels off from the experience."

"Did these come with an image?"

"They came from what looked like a hole in the floor of space."

"What associations do you make with that?"

I thought for a moment. "I remember reading an article a few years ago in a science magazine. That everything we see is made from the same particles that came from a black hole in space. The article surmised that the hole was God, the center of all creation. It left me with a lasting impression, so I think that's why it was showed to me that way."

She nodded, straightened her glasses, and read the first message out loud, "The evolution of your species has begun. The dawn of a new consciousness is here." She looked up at me. "I don't think there is any coincidence here that Dawn is your name."

"Yes, that struck me too. Oddly, my father named me. He told my mother that he had a dream that he was to name his first daughter 'Dawn'. He insisted on it."

"People are neither all bad nor all good," she said. "Even parts of your father were Divinely guided."

"Hard to believe."

She looked down at the journal and read again. "This is a delicate time. You need to take care of each other... It is very important to watch for the leaders because one is not real. He will have prejudices. Do not follow prejudice. This sounds like an anti-Christ message to me."

"It sounded like that to me too. Do not follow prejudice was heavily emphasized."

She nodded. "Do you think these are prophecies?"

"It struck me more like an announcement. Sound your trumpets a new beginning is here. And, apparently, I'm just the messenger. The first messenger. There will be others as we transition."

"What do you think we are transitioning to?"

"I think we are being liberated from the illusion of our separateness from each other and from God. The isolation, inadequacy and fear we feel will finally be over." I thought about the Kundalini energy and how that experience temporarily liberated me from my ego and how I felt such incredible love for strangers, knowing that I was them and they were me.

"I hope you're right. So, what else do the messages mean to you?" she asked.

"I think they mean what they say."

"Yes, and, if you are the messenger what about the messages are important to you?"

I looked out the window. What was still so vivid in my mind was the apocalyptic scene where so many people were rising from the earth, being annihilated in droves by something I couldn't see. "It all felt important. But the part about transforming our individual consciousness by choice... to use our current circumstance to heal. That's what sticks out for me."

"Why does that stick out?"

"It was clear that we have an opportunity right now to change the trajectory of humanity. And, I think we do that by taking personal responsibility for our healing. By following our own internal messages and bringing forth the Light within."

"Interesting. So that part of the message mirrors your journey. "

"It does?"

"Yes. You followed your messages, faced your fears, encountered great upheavals, and released a lifetime of stored emotions that, honestly, I'm surprised have not killed you by now. It's the hero's journey. You went through the crucible in order to come out the other side and bring back a treasure to the kingdom."

I thought about all the people that had helped me along the way. How fortunate I had been to afford professional care and help with my children. Despite the abuse, I lived a privileged life in a privileged community. How would others with lessor means be able to take such a journey. I looked at Judith.

"But most people don't have the means to go into therapy and take this kind of journey," I said. "I can afford this. What happens to all the people who can't?"

"It sounds like they return to their churches and synagogues for their healers."

"That part surprised me," I said. "When that message came out, I wanted to ask, 'are you sure?' But it was clear, this was not a dialogue with God. I was taking dictation."

"It makes sense," she said. "The soul is a self-healing organism. It is always trying to mend itself. Most people stay too busy to participate in their healing, until their anxiety or depression motivates them to seek treatment. Or they return to their churches or spiritual leaders to come back into alignment with themselves."

She looked back down at the journal.

"Learn to love now," she read. "What does that mean to you?"

"It seems to be the antidote to all of this. We need to focus on loving ourselves and others with real intention, and I think that will chase out everything that isn't love inside of us."

"You realize that is what you have been doing?"

"With Anne?"

"With Anne, with Jeff, the kids, even your father. You have loved them with all your heart, mind, and soul despite how they have injured you. And by loving them as deeply as you do, you have removed what isn't love inside of you," she said as she handed me back the journal.

"But now what? What am I supposed to do with this information? That apocalyptic vision I was shown was so horrific. Imagine turning on the TV and watching scenes where most of the people on earth are dying in droves. People have to know that we can stop that kind of suffering, that there is time for a gentle change."

"Then put it in your book," she said. "I'm sure that's why you were told to write it."

"But this book doesn't have an ending. I received the messages, and I now know that is what this calling has been all about, but I still don't feel whole. And, I haven't seen my soul in Anne's."

She nodded. "Are you still looking at her picture?"

"Yes, and I can't tell you what I see in her, but something is growing inside of me, and it feels like the love I have for her is who I am. And the stronger it becomes, the more I know in my heart that I will see her again."

"The love you feel for her is who you are. She was the mirror and you saw your true soul's reflection in her. You just have not fully owned it yet."

"That might be the case, but this journey isn't over until I see her again."

"Then why don't you go out and find her. I'm sure with your resources you could track her down and get an ending to your book."

"I'm sure I could, and I've thought about it. But if I try to control this, all I'm going to find is disappointment."

"Probably."

"So, I have to wait," I said. "I have to have faith and wait for my ending."

CHAPTER THIRTEEN

Katie was sitting cross legged on the couch gripping her cup of tea.

"Mom this is huge. Those messages are profoundly important, especially for my generation."

"It is profound. And yes, I know how important they are. I have struggled with how to communicate them for years."

"Do you think that's what's happening now?"

I nodded. "I think what is happening now is a macro version of the stages that I went through. Everything that needs to be healed is rising to the surface of our conscious minds."

She put down her teacup on the coffee table then leaned towards me.

"That scene that you saw of the souls rising from the earth. Do you think that vision could have been the Covid virus?"

"I think Covid is a shot over the bow. The vision I was shown was much worse than this virus. But we have time to change that trajectory. That's what was most significant about the messages to me."

"This makes me never want to have children."

"On the contrary. We need to raise strong children who can help us transition safely. But we need to nurture the souls in our children and let them be who they are being born to be, not hurt, neglect, or abuse them. It takes so much energy to recover from abuse. We can't afford to lose the hearts and minds of our children. We won't make it without them."

She nodded. "Good because I really do want to have kids."

"And I can't wait to love them."

"So was the calling to write the book?"

"It was to write the story I was living and share the messages."

She looked down at the manuscript on the table. "Is this it?"

"Yes. I self-published it and sold a few hundred copies. But it never really went anywhere. I prayed for direction and the only thing I ever received was to focus on raising you kids. So maybe it just wasn't time yet."

"Who sent this to you?"

I looked down at the hand-written note that was paper-clipped to the manuscript.

"Judith. I sent this to her over 20 years ago."

"What does the note say."

I read it out loud. "I remember your visions, and I think it's happening now. Hope you and your family are well. Love Judith."

"Wow. When was the last time you saw her?"

"Probably 20 years ago."

She looked down at the manuscript.

"Can I have this?"

"Sure."

She pulled the papers towards her and started skimming through the first chapter.

"Did you ever see Anne again? Did you see your soul in hers?"

"I did see Anne. But more importantly, I saw myself and connected to something I will never lose again.

ૐ

It happened a few months after I received the messages. Just before you kids went back to school. I was writing in my journal one morning and the message popped out.

Go to the big trees.

I didn't pay much attention until I had the same experience the following morning.

Go to the big trees.

The thought of big trees made me think of the Big Sur coastline. That was where tall groves of redwoods met the mid-coast of California. But the biggest redwoods in California were in the Sequoia National Park, so I told Jeff about the message and asked if he wanted to take the kids and go to the Sequoia Forest.

"Sure, as long as Maxx can go," he said.

The kids were out of school the following Thursday and Friday, so we penciled in a four-day vacation and I called to find a hotel.

After I made the reservation, Laura came over. She popped through the front door, yelled for me and then came up stairs to find me in the loft.

"Where have you been?" I asked. "I haven't seen you around all week."

"I just got back from a poetry workshop up north. Remember the one I told you about?" I vaguely remember her saying something to me around the time Jeff got home.

"It was at the Esalen Institute. You would love this place," she said as she lifted up a catalog. "It has every kind of healing, human potential kind of workshop you could want. There are even a few classes on the Chakra system and Kundalini energy."

"I've had enough Kundalini energy to last a lifetime," I said. She dropped the catalog on my desk, and we went downstairs and had coffee.

"So, are you still writing the book?" she asked. "Yes, and I understand why I needed to write it now, but I don't have an ending yet. I still haven't seen my soul in Anne's eyes and who knows how that's going to happen."

"How do you want it to happen?"

"I don't really care. I just want it to be over. Jeff and I are taking the kids to the sequoias next week. Maybe I will get some clarity while we're gone."

We spent the next twenty minutes talking about her poetry workshop before she headed out to run the afternoon carpool. When she left, I walked back to the loft to work on my book. An hour later, Judith called. She wanted to reschedule our appointment that week for a later time in the day. We made the change. Then, I told her about the message.

"Judith, I keep waking up into the message to go to the big trees. It's happened to me a few times this week."

"Go to Esalen," she said.

"Esalen?"

I picked up the catalog Laura just left and turned over the cover to see a picture of the property perched on a bluff along the Big Sur coastline surrounded by a grove of tall, majestic redwoods trees.

"Why should I go to Esalen?" I asked.

"Anne's there."

My heart started to race. "What? How do you know?"

"We have a mutual friend who lives in Oregon. I was talking to her last week and she said Anne was just with her and now she's heading to Esalen."

"You're kidding?"

"No, apparently she's going for a month." There was a long pause. "Are you still there?"

"Yes, I'm still here. This is so strange."

Judith and I made an appointment for Wednesday. When we hung up, I looked through the Esalen catalog for a workshop that lasted a month. I found only one, a certification program for massage therapy that was scheduled to begin the following Sunday. Good, I had over a week to figure out what I needed to do.

I went downstairs and told Jeff about my conversation with Judith and the brochure Laura gave me to Esalen.

"Great. I'll take you there," he said.

"What?"

"Instead of going to the Sequoias next weekend, we'll take the motor home up the coast. We can drop you off at Esalen on Sunday, and I'll take the kids camping while you're there."

"You'd do that?"

"Sure, I'll take you wherever you need to go."

It was my answer. If there was a workshop open, I'd go next week. I walked back upstairs and called Esalen; they only had one spot left open that week in a course on intimacy, so I booked it. It was all happening so fast, each step feeling so right, I never once questioned what I was doing.

I called Laura that night and told her what had happened.

"If you're lucky," she said, "you'll be put in the Big House. It's right on the cliff looking over the ocean. You might want to call and request it."

I didn't feel the need to call. At that point I was living on faith. "Do I need to bring a sleeping bag?"

"No, the rooms have bedding and towels, but they don't have phones. Tell Jeff if he wants to reach you, he will have to call the office and they will leave a message on the message board."

I thanked her, hung up, and went down to make dinner.

My fear didn't set in until I crawled into bed. Would she really be at Esalen? And if she was, what would it be like to see her again?

231

I turned over in bed and reached for Jeff's hand. "I hope I'm doing the right thing," I said.

He wove his fingers through mine. "You are. She was the closest thing to a real mother to you. But maybe this will give you a chance to see her as a person."

"I wonder what that will look like."

"I don't know, but I think you need to find out."

I prayed hard that night. I prayed that somehow she knew I was coming. That she could receive a message herself so my reunion with her would be the happy occasion I needed it to be.

I awoke early the next morning, and my chest began to bubble with an urgency to write. I picked up my journal and the message spewed out, as it had in the past--a stream of automatic writing.

> *She knows you're coming. She's ready to heal her heart. Spend time with her. You will heal her as she heals you. Let the Light work through you. Let the Light in and give it to Anne. You are meant to heal her as she heals you. Remember, you were meant and sent to heal her.*

I shook my head as I took down the message. Could this path get any stranger? I closed my journal and lay back in bed, feeling humbled by the information, wondering how any of that was going to happen.

Jeff woke up and I crawled under his arm; his touch was softer now, his advances less aggressive. He was sober every day and I had never known such consistency. I moved up on his chest and kissed him on the neck when the kids broke through the door and jumped in our bed.

"We're starved. Can we have some pancakes?"

Jeff moaned while I slowly got out of bed and took the kids to the kitchen.

On Wednesday, I went to my session with Judith. I sat down in my chair, my legs bouncing up and down on the floor as I told her about the month-long massage class, I thought Anne might be taking and the workshop on intimacy I'd reserved for myself.

Her face turned pale as she shook her head. "I don't know. That doesn't sound right. My friend never said anything about Anne being interested in bodywork. And maybe my dates were wrong. I don't know. Was it going to be this soon?"

"Judith, you sounded so clear on the phone."

"I just don't remember if the workshop was a month or two months. I think it was two months... but I don't know."

Her confusion appeared layered. "What is going on with you? Are you concerned about me going up there?"

"No, that's not it. When we got off the phone, I questioned whether I should have told you. But this is such an unusual case. Most therapists don't leave their practice. And when they do, they have an address or phone number where they can be reached. I've tried other ways to help you close this relationship with Anne, but nothing else has worked. I know you need to see her for your process to be over."

"Then what's the problem?"

She looked at me for a moment. "I guess it's realizing that this is the end of your process." She took a deep breath. "Therapists are humans. We get attached to people too."

Tears welled in my eyes and she handed me a tissue and took one for herself as she quickly changed the subject.

"What's the best and worst thing that can happen to you at Esalen?" she asked.

The change of subject calmed me. "The best thing would be that I'm healed, Anne's healed, and the relationship is healed. And I guess the worst thing is that she somehow rejects me."

"She already has rejected you. She left, and you grew up on your own. You have yourself as an adult now, and what happened before can't happen again."

"It feels like it can."

"That's your five-year-old talking, and she has no business going up to Esalen to meet Anne. This is for you as an adult."

I sat up in my chair. "I can't take the five-year-old?"

"No, you can't," she said as she leaned towards me. "Dawn, that child needed the relationship with Anne in order to get your attention. She needed to love and trust somebody enough so that you could love and trust yourself. But she has you now. She doesn't need Anne and she doesn't need you to abandon her for Anne. Leave her at home."

"All right."

"How are you going to make sure she's not there?"

"I'll check in with myself often and imagine her home with my kids."

"Good, because I don't want to receive a call from you telling me you ended up on the floor at Esalen. I'm not going to drive up to Big Sur, pick you up, and take you to the hospital again. I'm going to tell you to send the five-year-old home and handle this like an adult."

I smiled at her. Her tough love never felt so good.

"Dawn, I want you to hear this. You are an adult. You can be hurt or disappointed, but nothing Anne says or does can devastate you. Leave the child at home--she doesn't belong there."

"I promise. But even my adult self wants her to be happy to see me."

She took a deep breath then leaned forward. "Okay, I probably shouldn't be telling you this either, but Anne consulted with me when you were her client. She had deep feelings for you that she didn't know how to handle as a therapist. She was painfully conflicted, and it is one of the reasons she left. I didn't agree with her leaving. I thought she was running away instead of working through the feelings that were coming up for her while she was working with you. Seeing you again will likely bring up that conflict, so be prepared for her to run away again. And remember, if she does, this was really never about her anyway. It's about you, the reflection of yourself you saw in her, and your capacity to love another. She can't take that from you. Nobody can."

The warning felt a little dire. But despite the lack of contact, I knew Anne cared for me and I knew in my heart she would be happy to see me.

That Friday, I started getting the kids ready for the upcoming trip while Jeff was downstairs with a gentleman from a recruiting company. He was signing the final contract with an executive search firm--another sign that our lives were finally getting back to normal.

"I'm going to walk Mr. Evan to his car and then take Maxx for a walk," he yelled from downstairs.

"Okay," I said as I counted out the twelve pairs of underwear Katie had packed for our four day vacation. I went into her drawer and tried to balance her wardrobe. I was ready to start on Matthew's clothes when the phone rang. I ran into my bedroom to answer it. All I could hear was sobbing.

"He's dead... he's dead!" Jeff wailed from his car phone.

I scanned my mind for the kids. They were home. They were safe.

"What happened?"

"Maxx was just hit by a car. It hit him hard. Oh, God, he's dead. I know he's dead."

"Where are you?"

"I'm in the car, I'm taking him to the vet, but Maxx isn't moving. He's dead! He's dead!"

I was starting to feel numb. "He's going to be okay, Jeff. Maxx is going to be okay. Take a couple of deep breaths and tell me where you're going."

"His tail moved! He wagged his tail!"

"He's telling you he's going to be all right. Maxx is going to be all right. Now where are you going, so I can meet you there?"

"No. No. Stay with the kids, and please don't tell them what happened."

Jen was standing next to me listening to the conversation.

"Are you sure you don't want me to meet you?"

"Yes, I'm sure. I'll call you when I get there."

Matthew and Katie walked into the room. "What's happening?" Matthew asked.

"Maxx was just hit by a car," Jen said.

Katie and Matthew broke into tears. I walked over and held them.

"Dad took Maxx to the hospital and the doctors are taking good care of him. Dad will call us as soon as he knows anything."

We spent the next hour huddled on the couch distracting ourselves by watching sitcoms. The phone rang and we all ran to answer it. I picked it up.

"Maxx is alive," Jeff said. "There are no broken bones, but he's having some trouble breathing from the shock. The doctors want to keep him overnight, and if he's okay tomorrow, we can take him home in the afternoon."

"He'll be okay, Jeff. I know he will."

"I think so, too, but it doesn't look like we'll be able to make the trip."

"That's fine. I'll cancel the motor home, and if Maxx is okay, I'll drive up on my own on Sunday."

We were all sleepless that night. Jeff called every hour to check on Maxx, and every time he closed his eyes, he saw him being hit by the car. "Maxx ran right into that car," he kept saying. "He ran right into it." He tossed and turned. "I should have had him on a leash. Why didn't I have him on a leash?"

I fell asleep just before dawn, and when I awoke, Jeff was gone. He called after breakfast to say that Maxx was standing up. His breathing was still labored, but he could walk.

"I slept in his kennel with him," Jeff said. "I chewed on his ear to make sure he knew who I was."

"Maxx knows who you are, Honey."

"I'm going to stay here for awhile. I don't want Maxx to be alone."

"Okay, I'm going to cancel the motor home and see if we can get back our deposit."

"Dawn, I still want you to go to Esalen. I know it's important. You have to go."

"We'll see."

Jeff came home for lunch and went straight to bed. I had put away the kids' clothes and was heading down to clean the kitchen when the phone rang. I picked up before it woke Jeff.

"Hello."

"This is Doctor Klein, the veterinarian. Maxx is having some real trouble breathing and I'd like to send him to another facility where they can put in a chest tube until we can assess the lung damage."

Jeff picked up the other phone halfway through the conversation. "I'll be right there," he said. He ran out of the house without saying goodbye.

"Is Maxx going to be okay?" Matthew asked.

"Yeah, Maxx will be okay. Whatever happens, Maxx will be okay."

I finished cleaning the kitchen, and we went to buy groceries. The kids were in good spirits as they ran down the aisles. My pace was slower, my chest filled with trepidation. I bought them the ice cream sandwiches I usually denied and, sensing my weakness, they pushed for some gum. My bill was twenty dollars more than it normally was, but my kids were happy and relatively quiet.

We had loaded the groceries and were headed back home when Jeff's van pulled up next to me at the light. His shoulders were shaking, and he was hunched over the steering wheel. He looked over at me and mouthed the words.

"He didn't make it," he said. "He didn't make it."

I looked at him and moaned. Maxx had been everything to Jeff. His emotional support, his companion. How could this happen to him? I shook my head as tears streamed down my face. I would have given up my chance of ever seeing Anne again, if God would have just brought back his dog.

In the morning, Isabella fed the kids breakfast, while Jeff slipped Maxx's dog tags in his pocket and we left for the beach. We walked a few miles down the bike path to a bench at the edge of a bluff that hung a hundred feet above the rolling deep blue waters. Jeff was rubbing the silver dog tags between his hands as we sat down. He could barely speak, breaking into tears, until he finally collapsed his head into my chest. I held him tightly.

"I should have never let him off his leash," he cried.

"It was an accident, Honey. It's not your fault."

"It happened so fast. I... I... didn't see it coming."

I pulled him closer and he started to sob.

"I miss him so much," he said in a voice so small, so broken, I could tell he wasn't just talking about Maxx anymore. He was talking about his dad.

"What am I going to do without him?"

His breath was short and shaky as his tears poured onto my shirt.

"I don't know. But we're going to get through this. We are going to get through this together."

He stayed in my arms through waves of tears until he was finally able to catch his breath.

"I can't do it," he said. "I thought I could throw his dog tags in the water to say goodbye, but I can't do it."

"Then don't. Hold on to those tags and remember how much you love him. You never have to let him go in your heart."

He sat up, our hands still clasped as we looked over the ocean.

"What a journey this has been," he said.

"Yes, it has and it needs to be over. I can't leave now. I think it's best if I stay home with you and the kids."

"You have to go to Esalen."

"I don't want to go anymore. You and the kids are so much more important than anything that could happen up there."

He turned and looked into my eyes. "You have to go. I need you to go. You are not going to stop searching until you do."

"What if everything I need is right in front of me."

"It is, but you are not going to find that out until you go there."

"But what about you and the kids?"

"We'll be fine. Isabella and I will play with them the whole time."

I rested my head on his shoulder, and we looked out to sea. I thought about the void Maxx was going to leave in his life, and how much I wanted to be the one to fill it.

He grabbed my hand and pulled me up from the bench.

"Come on. Let's go home and talk to the kids."

We walked down the side of the bluff, took off our shoes and jumped onto the sandy beach still moist from the receding tide. The waves lapped at our feet as the sun began to chase away the morning chill. We strolled around the point and onto the half-moon shaped cove when Jeff dropped my hand.

"Oh my God," he said as he peered out over the waves.

"What?"

"Do you see it?" he said as he ripped off his shirt and threw it down on the sand.

"See what?"

He ran into the water and jumped over a wave, then swam through the next one as he headed toward a reef. Just before the rock, a small brick-red buoy appeared. Jeff grabbed the buoy, held it up to the sky and yelled. "Thank you, Maxx. Thank you!"

CHAPTER FOURTEEN

I loaded the refrigerator with casseroles and desserts, trying to anticipate Jeff and the kids needs while I was gone,
trying to feel less guilty about leaving. After breakfast on
Sunday, I said goodbye to the kids and checked in with my
inner five-year-old. I imagined her on the couch eating pop-
sicles with Matthew and asked her to stay with him and not
creep into my consciousness while I was gone. For the next
week, I would need to be an adult.

Jeff walked me out to the van and loaded my bag. It still
smelt like Maxx.

I leaned over and gave him a kiss goodbye. "I'm coming
back, you know."

He smiled, "I know."

I listened to the radio up the coast, the music drowning
out any thoughts of my own. When I hit the center of the
state, I turned off the music and focused my attention on the
change in scenery. The ocean below the rocky cliffs was calm,
hugging the coast like a big blue blanket as the van tilted
around the curves of the winding coast highway. I swerved
into fog banks and then back into sunshine, the extremes
feeling much like my thoughts.

The fog dissipated and the tall, majestic redwoods now
lined the highway. Brilliant hues of deep greens and blues

painted the landscape as towering trees jetted up from jagged cliffs, backlit by the sun bouncing off the ocean. The crisp cool air coming through the vents was as invigorating as the epic scenery. Around every turn was another expansive view of the ocean. I took it all in as it lightened my spirits. The scenery speaking to my soul like a return to home.

According to the map, I was near and began to focus on the road signs. Laura had warned me that the entrance was easy to miss. Several more turns around hairpin bends and a small wooden sign appeared that read *Welcome to Esalen.*

My heart started to race as I pulled down the steep gravel driveway to the parking attendant sitting next to a wooden booth. A middle-aged man with his hair tucked behind his ears directed me to the registry.

I stepped out of the van and looked around deeply inhaling the fresh pine and salt air. On the edge of the property overlooking the ocean was a brilliant green lawn that sprawled through the grounds, each blade of grass calling notice to its life. I walked past some pine trees and out to the cliff. Below me was the majestic Big Sur coastline: steep curves of jagged rock embraced by the pliable blue waters that foamed white at its borders. A lone bird glided down a wind current; from below came the bark of an otter.

I walked through the vegetable garden and over to the office feeling nervous yet strangely at peace. Everything in nature told me she was there. Everything around me seemed part of who I was.

I walked to the counter and gave the clerk my name. I thought of asking about Anne, but then my attention was drawn to the computer behind the clerk. Taped to the monitor was a handwritten note: *TRUST.* I heeded the message.

The clerk handed me my keys. "You're in the Big House," he said. "Here's a map to your room and the schedule for your workshop."

I walked past the garden and over a walking bridge that was dampened by the mist of a nearby waterfall, then turned down a path to the Big House, a large, country-style home that stood on the cliff. A red brick patio surrounded the house, and redwoods with roots that curved above the ground extended high above the arch of the two-story building. My room was upstairs, a small bedroom at the beginning of the hall with an old, wooden desk against one wall and two twin beds pushed up against two windows that looked out over the ocean. I put down my luggage and opened the windows; the sounds of the ocean poured in with the fresh air.

There was no sign of a roommate, so I put away my stuff and walked to the cafeteria to get something to eat. On the way, I checked the message board, a piece of framed cork that hung outside the office. There was nothing with Anne's name on it, but there was a message for me. I pulled it down and opened it. The message was from Laura.

No one can fail who seeks to reach the truth.

-A Course in Miracles-

Love,
Laura

Warmed by her kindness, I put the note in my pocket and went in for dinner. The cafeteria was a rustic lodge with benches lining a window that overlooked the pool. In the rear of the room was a lounge area, a raised platform with sitting pillows sprawled around wooden coffee tables. I went through the buffet line and sat by the window. There was no sign of Anne.

I ate three bites of stew, pushed away my plate and pulled out the schedule for my workshop. The first session was to begin at eight that night, and would meet for two hours every morning, afternoon and evening. Wednesday was the only night I had free.

I looked at my watch, a quarter to seven. Outside the kitchen was a pile of dirty dishes. I added my plate and walked outside. The air was brisk and still, the night too dark to see. I turned on my flashlight and walked back to my room. A duffel bag was on the other bed and a light jacket hung in the closet.

At eight o'clock, I went downstairs to the unfurnished living room where my group was scheduled to meet. The workshop leaders greeted us warmly at the door: Ted, a handsome man in his early forties wearing jeans and a button-down shirt, and Gina, a gray-haired, full-bodied dark-skinned woman wearing a sea-green, long sweater and flowing, ankle-length skirt.

Inside the door were stacks of pillows. Each of us grabbed one as we entered and sat down in a large circle on the carpet. I sat next to a man who looked like Jay Leno. He smiled warmly as he firmly shook my hand.

"Hi, I'm Paul."

I introduced myself and we greeted the people around us. So far, there were about twenty of us, men and women from all over the world.

Ted and Gina gave a brief introduction of the intimacy workshop, then asked each of us to share why we had decided to take the course. The floor opened to Paul.

"I was supposed to come here with my wife," he said, "but she couldn't make it. We've been married for fifteen years and would like to find ways to have a more intimate relationship." He finished and turned to me.

I wasn't about to say that I picked the course on a whim so I could find my old therapist and instead shared I had been dealing with childhood abuse issues and quickly turned to the person next to me.

When group was over, I went up to my room. My roommate, who was taking the same workshop, walked in behind me. She introduced herself as Catherine, a bubbly, middle-aged therapist with long, curling, red hair, who worked with troubled teenagers in a high school in Massachusetts. We hit it off right away. By midnight, we were as comfortable as sisters.

In the morning, Catherine and I met Paul in the lobby and the three of us went up for breakfast. I hadn't slept much. Every step toward the cafeteria was making me more nervous. We stopped at the message board so I could put up a note for Anne. I wanted to let her know I was there, give her some time before she saw me.

I posted the note, and we went and sat down to eat. I was full after a few bites and my heart fluttered every time the door opened. If Anne was there, she would have to come here to eat, and in two meals I hadn't seen her. By the end of breakfast, I had a headache. To hell with trust. I needed the facts. I excused myself from the table and walked into the office.

"Excuse me," I said to the clerk. "I think a friend of mine is here. Could you check for her on the roster?"

"Sure, what's her name?"

"Anne Myers."

"That name sounds familiar." He grabbed a clipboard and scanned through the workshops.

"No... No, I don't see her. But I recognize the name. I think she left yesterday."

The lump in my throat dropped into my stomach. I'd missed her by one day?

"I'm sorry. Is there something else I can do for you?" he asked.

"No. Thank you." I put on my sunglasses, walked out the door and tore my note to her off the message board. One day. How could I have missed her by one day?

I walked down to a rock on the lawn. Everything around me was still telling me she was there. *Shut up!* I screamed to the voice in my head. The same voice that told me that Maxx was okay. Maxx is dead and Anne's not here.

I walked over the bridge, past the big yellow house, and down a flight of stairs onto a rocky beach. I threw off my jacket and picked up some stones.

"Damn it! I don't deserve this!" I burst into tears as I smashed the rocks into the water. "Why did Maxx have to die? And why did you bring me here?" I yelled to the sky. "Why?"

My tears turned to sobs as I sat on the rocks. "I don't want to be hurt anymore. Please. Please, let this be over."

The tears were still pouring down my face when I walked up to the group and joined the workshop. As we sat down in our circle, twenty-four pairs of eyes seemed to be staring at me. Ted addressed me as soon as the circle began.

"Dawn, this is a sacred circle, and it's safe if you want to share what's happening." I was so present in my emotions I couldn't control them.

"I saw this therapist," I cried, "whom I loved very deeply. She was helping me through sexual abuse memories from my childhood and I came to trust and love her very much. But about a year after I started seeing her, she quit her practice and left the country." There was gasp in the room.

"We were very close, and we never had closure. Last week, I heard she was here and the only reason I came up to take this class was so I could find her." My voice cracked as the woman next to me reached for my hand. "I asked for her at the desk this morning and they said I had missed her by one day."

The group winced.

"I'm sorry, Dawn." Ted, the workshop leader said. "I'm really very sorry."

I took a breath and composed myself. Gina, the other workshop leader addressed me warmly. "Dawn," she said, "the exercise this morning is to talk about the strength that enabled us to survive our childhood. Would you like to start?"

I wiped my eyes. "Hope. Hope enabled me to survive my childhood. The hope that someday there would be an answer. That the world would somehow, someday, make sense. But I'm giving up on hope. Faith is driving me crazy, and I don't want to hear it in my head anymore."

A sigh of sadness echoed in the room. I looked at Paul to take the attention off myself, and he picked up the question and it went around the circle. I listened to stories of people who survived on good behavior, on rebellion, and as caretakers to their parents. There were people who survived by running away and people who survived by submission. Each voice spoke a part of my truth. I had been all of them, just as they had been me.

When our morning session was over, we walked up for lunch. The anticipation of seeing Anne was finally over and the relief brought back my appetite. I loaded up a plate and went outside to eat with Catherine. It was a clear, warm day and the dry air made me thirsty. I set down my plate, downed a glass of water and went back to the cafeteria for another cup. While I was filling my glass from the spigot, a woman who resembled Anne walked by. Her tennis shoes and leggings were worn, the sleeves on her green sweatshirt were pushed up to her elbows. I stared at her back as she walked toward a table, holding my breath squinting for recognition. Was it Anne? She crossed the room slowly, appearing taller than I remembered Anne, her gait more confident. The woman's long, brown hair covered her face as she put down her plate. Then she turned to sit. I saw her face clearly. It was Anne. A smile returned to my face that I hadn't felt in years.

My mind went blank as I walked up to her chair.

"Hi," I said as I stood in front of her.

She looked up at me and slowly nodded. "I always knew I was going to see you again."

I just stared at her in disbelief.

She took a bite of her salad. "Sit down," she said, gesturing to the empty seat beside her.

I dropped down in the chair, my hands trembling. "I can't believe I'm seeing you. They told me at the desk you weren't here."

"I got here yesterday. But I'm in a residence program. They probably checked the workshops." She took another bite.

"What's the residency program?"

"It's a therapy program, and it's accredited by the state so I can use it for further training as a therapist. We work in the different maintenance departments during the day and we go to therapy groups at night. I think I'm in the laundry this week."

My stomach started to quiver, and she reached for my hand.

"It's okay. I knew I was going to see you again. And I just had to trust that when it was right the universe would somehow bring us back together."

"How do you two know each other?" said the man to her left.

"Dawn, this is Uray. He's a friend of mine."

"Hi, Uray." I looked back at Anne. I told her about the message to go to the big trees and the sequence of events that had brought me to Esalen.

She listened, cautiously amused. Still eating her plate of salad that sat on the rustic, dark, wooden table.

"I'm working here," she said, "I'm not sure how much time we will have to spend together, but you're welcome to come eat with us, and on Wednesday night I don't have a session. We can get together then."

"That's good. I don't have a workshop on Wednesday night either." My body was still shaking. "I think I need some time to let this sink in," I said.

She nodded and I stood up and hugged her. Her embrace was short and rigid.

"It's good to see you," I said.

Her eyes began to warm. "It's good to see you, too."

"It was nice to meet you," I said to Uray. It was the first time we made eye contact. He was tall and blonde with a boy's pale, soft skin face in a man's broad-shouldered body.

"Nice to meet you," he said with an accent I couldn't distinguish.

I walked back to the Big House laughing at myself--at how my lack of trust brought on so much of my own suffering. I saw Catherine on the path that went through the garden and as we walked back to our room. I told her about Anne.

"Was it strange? Was it awkward? Was she glad to see you?"

"Yes, yes and yes."

"Are you going to see her again?"

"Wednesday night we're going to meet. But I'll probably see her before then." I took off my jacket and picked up a towel. "Do you want to go to the hot springs with me?" I asked.

"I'd love to, but I have some things I need to read."

I walked back over the bridge and past the garden. In front of the cafeteria, I ran into Anne. Uray was a few feet away.

"Hi," I said. "I'm going to the hot springs. Do you want to come?"

She hesitated. "I just found out I have the afternoon off, but I told Uray I would help him clean some rooms."

"Are you sure? I have a lot to tell you."

She looked back at him. He looked like a little boy who didn't want his mom to go. "I don't know," she said. There was a long pause. "Okay, I'll meet you down there."

I waited for Anne at the front of the bathhouse, in awe that I was finally seeing her, relieved that I would have the chance to share with her all the things that had happened.

She walked up a few minutes later, and we went down to the baths, large tubs made of smooth, gray stones that stood on a deck, perched from the jagged cliffs high above the coastline. The hot springs were bathing suit optional—and no one I saw opted for a suit. I was embarrassed to think that I was about to be naked with my old therapist, but she seemed so comfortable taking off her clothes that I quickly adapted and felt very comfortable too. The sun was nearing the horizon, as we stepped into the tubs, the ocean was as calm as a morning sea.

Anne sat next to me. Being naked next to her felt so vulnerable and real. The most honest and open environment I think I had ever experienced.

"This is a pretty good place for God to bring us back together," she said.

"Divine perfection," I said.

I gushed on about the journey I had been on. I shared that her leaving had helped me access and release the stored emotions from my childhood. Then I told her about the messages I received over the three nights in May and how imperative it is that we learn to love ourselves and others now. I started to share more details, but none of what I was saying seemed to be connecting, so I calmed myself down and looked at her.

She smiled at me as if she was enjoying the silence. We sat motionless for several minutes, then a bright light reflected off the water and up into her face. For a moment, I was blinded by the glare, and when my vision cleared--her body appeared translucent and sitting across from me was a loving, compassionate spirit, softly glowing at me as if I was looking into a mirror. The sight brought words to my mouth that felt as if they were given to me. Words I later realized I was saying to myself.

"You were love and faith to me," I said, "and everybody kept telling me I wasn't going to see you again, but I knew that I would. And now that I have, I am never going to lose you again." The sound of an otter came up from the ocean below and I suddenly fell from the realm of my own reflection, not yet able to fully make it my own.

Anne shook her head. "No, I knew I would see you again. I knew you thought I was just another person in your life who screwed you over, but every time I talked to my friends about calling you, they just kept telling me I had to let it go." She shook her head. "But it never felt right. I knew there was something about our relationship that just didn't translate into words, but if you hear something enough times you start to realize there's probably a reason for it."

I told her about the book I received and the Tibetan practice of placing a teacher with a student until the student saw his or her soul in the teacher. And how I had used her picture to try and connect to that part of myself.

She leaned back against the tub. "I gave you a picture?"

"Yes, you did."

"What picture did I give you?"

"You were holding a rabbit."

"I was?"

I felt like I had been punched in the gut. I splashed some water over my face. How could she have forgotten about the picture? I took a deep breath and checked in with my body. My heart was hurt and I suddenly felt very alone. The reality that she meant a lot more to me, than I did to her, was sinking in quickly.

"I guess I'm just having an unusual life," I said.

"You really are."

"Anyway, enough about me. Are you alright?" I asked.

"Yeah, I really am. I've had a lot of fun the past two years. I came back from Australia, bought a van, and camped all through the West. It's been great."

"Did you come here with Uray?"

"Yes, but he's just a friend. I met a man from Germany about a year ago. We traveled through Canada together. And then we were scheduled to come here, but his visa ran out and they wouldn't let him cross the border back into the States." She took a deep breath. "It's really hard to be here without him."

"What's his name?"

"Otto."

I nodded. "Next time, I'm taking your path. It sounds a lot more fun than the one I've been on."

"It hasn't been all fun. It's really hard living with somebody in a van, and there are some issues with Otto that I came here to work on." She turned on a blast of cool water, then moved closer to me.

"How's therapy going?" she asked.

"Good. I've spent a lot of time working on my transferences with you. And I was told you probably had a few with me."

"They told you that, did they?"

I smiled at her. "Yes, they did."

"It's true. I had some issues that came out in our relationship that were part of my own process."

"What were your transferences?" I asked.

The energy changed. She was letting down and becoming more comfortable with me.

"You were absolutely a daughter to me. And I knew what my leaving was going to put you through. Believe me, I know how much that hurt you." Her eyes filled with tears. I stepped over and held her and she welcomed the embrace. The energy between us felt very natural, feminine, void of any sexual feelings or tension.

"I received a message," I said. "A few days before I came here. It said you were ready to heal your heart."

"Oh, yes," she cried, "yes... yes. I have worried and wondered about you for a very long time."

Another wave of tears came up from her chest. I held her tightly, my senses fully present.

"It's okay," I said.

She pulled away. "I know it is."

I sat back and went inward. I felt the tension of her push-pull, as if something about me was threatening to her.

A group of people joined us in the tub. We got out and walked to a vacant one.

I slowly picked up my towel. I was still feeling hurt from her not remembering she gave me her picture and I wanted to leave.

"I'm feeling kind of stuck," I said. "Maybe I should go back to my group."

She sat down in another tub. "Or you could stay here and just be stuck."

I accepted her invitation and climbed in the tub. I had come all this way. I might as well tell her how I felt.

"I know we had different experiences of each other," I said, "but part of mine was that I came to love you very deeply."

"You really did, didn't you?"

"Yes, I did, and I know that was my own experience."

She nodded. "Isn't that all life is? Our own experience of it?"

I wished I hadn't stayed.

"I guess, but it's lonely to think I was in it alone."

"You weren't in it alone. And I don't think the love I experienced with you was any more or less. It was just different."

"How's that?"

"I knew from the first days we worked together that I had always loved you. I don't know in what past life or what relationship and I don't need to know. But I have always loved you and always will."

Her words were soothing. I splashed some more water on my face and leaned back against the hot tub wall.

"What's going on with you and Jeff?" she asked.

"Jeff's a good man. I just thought that if I could somehow get my heart open through my relationship with you, it would then be open for him. I don't know if that makes sense anymore. But I used to think it did."

"So, what do you need from me?"

"I need to free myself. To let go of my fears in your arms so I can let my soul back in my body."

She smiled. "I think we might be able to arrange that this week." She pointed to the sun as it touched the horizon, yellow and orange glowing from its borders. We waded to the edge of the tub and she put her arm around me. "It's beautiful, isn't it?"

"Yes, it is."

I let go of my thoughts and reached for her hand, feeling how safe I was in her arms. I then closed my eyes, and saw the Light in my mind, and instead of feeling afraid, I let go of all resistance and let the Light in. A slow flood of energy began filling my body like warm liquid pouring into an empty glass. It filled my chest and rose through the top of my head overflowing like a fountain down the outside of my skin. Suddenly every cell in my body felt alive. I was being reborn in that moment, my soul fully incubated into life. With a slight gasp, I took what felt like my first breath of air. Air that was lighter and fresher than I thought air could be.

"I'm glad you came," she said. "You have given me a very healing gift."

I nodded, moving my hand slightly, just enough to feel the skin on her fingers, just enough to feel her skin on my own.

I basked in the peace as the sun disappeared. Then as the stars began to appear, I remembered that I was still on a mission. I was to receive the Light and give it to Anne.

"It feels like there's something else I'm supposed to give you," I said.

"I don't know what that could be. You've already given me plenty."

Another person entered the hot tub and we got up and toweled off.

"I have to run," she said, "but I'm sure I will see you sometime tomorrow."

She left quickly to meet up with somebody while I meandered down the path to the Big House to catch the last minutes of my workshop. The word had spread that I'd found Anne, and when I entered the living room I was greeted with cheers.

"You look like a lit candle," said a woman from Missouri.

Paul came up and hugged me. "You're beautiful."

"Thank you. It was a good reunion." I said as my body maintained its peaceful state of being.

I went to bed that night elated, and shortly after I awoke the next day, my fears began to return. I had been wide open with Anne, exposed the way a small island is to the elements that surround it. Our relationship, now more than ever, was too intense to be causal. Until I could ground myself in the awareness of my own soul, in the feelings of wholeness I felt in her arms, I needed to avoid her. I went to the cafeteria early, ate fast, then took a walk with Catherine.

We came back for the morning group, and Gina ran the session, teaching us a physical exercise of positioning designed to help us be aware of whether we preferred to dominate or be submissive. Domination felt too aggressive. Submission was frightening.

Before lunch, I grabbed a towel from the laundry. I knew Anne worked there. Her work program included doing the laundry and cleaning rooms, and my heart was pounding as I walked up to the small building. I reached the door and, from the corner of my eye, saw Anne duck into the back. Oh shit--she was avoiding me. My heart began to race as if trying to run away from me; the despair opening in my chest was threatening to swallow me whole. I went to the bridge to regroup. This was not happening. This could not be happening. It was just my imagination--I needed to try again.

When I came back to the laundry room, she was folding some towels. I walked up and stood beside her, trying to say something clever, but nothing clever came out. Her attempts at small talk were as impaired as mine. Then, as if trying to spare us the pain of an awkward situation, she turned and pulled me into a long, very loving embrace. In her arms there was no confusion. I was sitting in my own soul connected to hers. I walked away feeling whole and at peace again. Moments later, thinking of how she tried to avoid me, the wholeness vanished into a feeling of rejection. My five-year-old was creeping back in.

I took a hot tub and caught her at the tail end of lunch.

"I have to leave in five minutes," she said. "Uray and I have a room to clean."

I sat down. Anne began to tell me a story about a guru in San Francisco--how he had discouraged one of his students who idolized him. She left before I had a chance to tell her, I didn't think of her as a guru. Nor did I idolize her.

Tuesday night's dinner was in the same vein as lunch. I ate with my group and we celebrated a birthday. Anne was across the room in the lounge talking with friends. When we finished our cake, I walked over to see her. She smiled warmly and made room for me on her pillow.

"Sit down," she said, "but I have to leave in two minutes."

She introduced me to the woman across from us, then with a burst of energy took me into her arms. I put my head on her chest and wrapped my arms around her waist, and in a surge of love that felt as though it lit our corner of the room, my disappointment vanished.

I was wondering what the woman across from us must be thinking when I was pulled in by a sound that made the room disappear. Against Anne's chest I began to hear the deep purring of small, subtle, pleasure moans that stopped as she inhaled and released with her breath.

I lost myself in her rhythm. The love within me was so exquisite my body no longer felt structured. I softly pulled in on her waist and began to perceive it as my own; suddenly my ego boundary was gone and we were no longer separate. I was holding my own soft, rounded, compassionate soul--feeling its bliss, listening to its pleasure--its satisfaction that I had returned.

"This feels like home," I said.

She squeezed me tightly, then whispered in my ear, "Uray's standing over there waiting for me. I'm sorry. I have to go."

I sat up and said good-bye. I was aware that I had received something in that embrace, but I was still unaware of what it was. I walked back to my group with Catherine and

Paul. We stopped by the message board, as I saw one with my name.

> *Live each present moment completely and the future will take care of itself.*

> *Love,*
> *Laura*

On Wednesday morning, as I was finishing breakfast, Anne walked in. I poured some tea and sat next to her. She tensed with a hint of annoyance, dug her fork into her boiled egg and twisted out the yolk. I struggled to decide which would be more awkward--getting up and leaving or staying next to her. A man from her group came up and sat down. She introduced us and left.

I passed Uray on the path twice that day. He glared at me out of the corner of his eye, like a little boy guarding the border of a hostile land. I wanted to slap him. Tell him he was about as intimidating as a bug on the bottom of my shoe. But I didn't need to add to the tension, so I ignored him and went about my day. The hours were now passing slowly. I assumed Anne was still planning to meet me that night, so I spent the afternoon down on the beach, telling myself that whatever was happening with her was about her, and not about me.

I ate dinner that night with some people from my workshop, spending the meal poking at my food. Anne walked in with Uray. They filled their plates and sat down across the room. I couldn't stand the wait, so I asked Paul for his towel and got up to go to the hot tubs. I walked up to Anne to tell her where I'd be, but before I could open my mouth she snapped, "Do you mind. We're eating. I'll meet you when we're finished."

Her tone was so harsh, I felt like I'd been slapped in the face.

"I just wanted to ask what time we were meeting so I could go down to the hot tubs."

She looked at her watch. "I'll meet you back here in forty-five minutes."

I walked out in a daze. I wasn't sure what God had in mind when He sent me to her, but I sure didn't deserve to be treated that way.

I went down and sat in the tubs. Twenty minutes later, Uray walked in, took off his clothes and took the furthest hot tub from me. He glared in my direction, now looking like a tall-boy protecting his mother. I assumed he was to be my sign that Anne was ready so I stayed in the hot springs for another twenty minutes.

I walked back to the cafeteria and sat down next to Catherine. Anne walked up a few minutes later.

"Are you ready?" she asked.

"Yes."

I felt as though I was going to a showdown, neither of us talking as we walked out on to the lawn and down to a pair of large rocks. Anne sat on one while I sat on the ground and leaned against the other.

"What is going on with you?" I asked.

"What do you mean?"

"The push pull. One minute you love me, the next minute you want me to get the hell out of here."

She nodded. "I admit there has been some of that, but that's because I didn't know what kind of relationship I wanted to have with you when you left here. But I have clarity now, and when you leave here on Friday, I want to say goodbye to you."

"That's fine."

"It is?"

"Yes, it is. Anne, I have a husband and three children to go home to. I didn't come up here to try to attach myself to you. And to tell you the truth, I hadn't even thought about what our relationship would be like when I left here."

She looked confused. "When you said the other night that you were never going to lose me again, it sounded like you had thought about it."

"What I'm never going to lose again is what I saw in you. And I needed to hear myself say that. What kind of relationship we have when I leave here seems to be irrelevant to why I'm here."

"Then I should probably back up. Why are you here?"

I set back my shoulders. "I told you. I got the message to go to where you were. That we were to spend time together. That it was time to heal your heart and that when the Light came through you to me, I was supposed to give it back to you. Anne, I didn't take this path, this path took me."

"I don't buy that. We all hear many voices. It was your choice to act on them."

"No, Anne, it is not the voice you think. I'm not a child anymore."

"I'm not so sure about that."

I glared at her.

"That didn't come out right," she said. "I mean to the extent that none of us really grow up. I mean we all have stuff left over from our childhood. I know I do, and I know most of my friends do."

That was obvious.

"I know the information I received was real. I didn't make it up," I said.

"I didn't say you did. But that sounded a little like you were trying to convince yourself."

I thought the frustration was going to split my head open. Throughout my journey, it was the closest I had come to feeling as though I was truly going to lose my mind. I pulled at the roots of my hair and stared up at the sky, the stars twinkling their message. *Steady, steady, steady, all is well, as it's supposed to be.*

"What's with the hair pulling?" she asked.

I stood up and snapped at her. "Why did God have to set me up with you? Why couldn't Jesus have come into my life? He's dead. He would have been easy to love. It's people that are a fuckin' nightmare, and loving you hasn't been easy."

She chuckled.

"More times than once I've wanted to rip you from my heart and get you the hell out of my life," I said.

"I know the feeling."

"But I knew I had to keep loving you. No matter what, I just had to keep loving you."

"But I keep hearing you say you want something from me. That you're trying to get something that I don't want to give."

"No, Anne, I told you that I knew this was my own experience."

She paused for a moment. "When is your workshop over?" she asked.

"Friday at noon."

"I break for lunch at noon," she said. "I'll meet you in the cafeteria. But if whatever this healing you think is supposed to happen between us doesn't happen by then, I still want to say goodbye to you."

"That's fine. I want to be free of this relationship as much as you do."

"Dawn, I'm already free of this relationship. And I don't think you understand that."

I nodded in disgust. *You might be free of me. But you're not free.*

She stood up to leave while I struggled to make sense of her ambivalence. "What were your transferences again?" I asked.

She looked annoyed. "I told you that the other day."

"Tell me again."

"I took you for a daughter."

There was more going on here than that. "Was this ever sexual for you?"

"No. Never."

"Then I don't know what your problem is," I said. "But I want you to know that I have never idolized you, and I have never thought of you as a guru. As far as I'm concerned, you're just as screwed up as I am."

She started to laugh, which softened the moment. I took a deep breath and calmed myself down.

"Anne, I know I dumped a bunch of stuff on you the other day in the hot tubs, but my intentions in coming here were pure."

She nodded. "This has been really hard for me, but I feel better now." She put her hands in her pocket and maintained an awkward distance between us.

"I gather this means you can't hug me anymore," I said.

She opened her arms, her embrace was rigid and cold. The night before I'd been taken to heaven. Tonight, the gates were closed.

I turned on my flashlight and we walked up the grass.

"I'm glad we got this settled," she said, "because I came here to work on another relationship and I really need to move on to those issues."

I shook my head and laughed at myself. I had been a fool for love. A tenacious, incorrigible fool.

"What's so funny?" she asked.

"Nothing. Nothing at all."

She asked me to walk her up the hill so she could use my flashlight to see the lock on her bike.

"Fridays are really busy around here," she said as she turned the combination. "I'll check my schedule, but I'm only going to have about twenty minutes to meet with you."

"Whatever, Anne. Whatever."

I went back to the hot springs. There was nobody in the tubs and the tranquility was comforting. I took off my clothes and stepped in the farthest one out on the patio, floating in the water looking up at the sky. The stars looked so peaceful I wanted to join them, become a light shining down on the drama, no longer a participant, simply an observer.

One of our workshop leaders, Ted, stepped into the hot tubs. "What are you doing out here alone?" he asked.

"Just looking at the stars."

We talked about hiking, the workshop, and Esalen. I didn't need to talk about Anne. I was hurt, but I wasn't devastated.

By the time I got back to my room, my apathy had worn off and anger had set in. Who the hell did she think she was, talking to me like a condescending parent, shoving me to the side so she could get on to something more important? I tossed and turned until Catherine walked in.

"How did it go?" she asked.

"I hate her."

"That bad, huh?"

"Yes, that bad." I told her what happened. Or, at least my version of it.

"Why do you think she slammed down a boundary like that?" she asked.

"Who knows."

"Why don't you ask her?"

I grabbed a pillow and held it over my lap. "No. I told her how much I loved her, and I think she thinks I want something from that."

"Do you?"

"I just wanted to be in the love long enough to ground it in myself. And I think that was happening. I feel like I am so close. I can see her soul. I can even feel it and I am getting glimpses of it being me, but then she takes off so fast I can't seem to hold on to the perception that the compassionate spirit I fell so deeply in love with is really my own. It's like my reflection keeps running away."

"Or maybe you are still running away from your reflection." Catherine said as she put on her nightshirt. "You were doing the right thing though. I work with teenagers, and the whole trick with them is to hold them steady within the boundaries while we give them a safe place to love. It sounds like Anne did that with you. It's too bad she couldn't follow it through."

"But she is a therapist. She must know what's happening. Why is she running?"

"Clearly the relationship brings up strong feelings for her she doesn't handle well. When you were in therapy, she was in control. She set the boundaries. But you are equals here, the other parts of who she is are exposed and it sounds like she might not be comfortable with that. Her role as therapist prevented her from fully being seen."

"But I did see her. And what I saw in her was so incredibly loving and beautiful."

"Just because you saw it in her, does not mean she sees it in herself. Sounds like she might be running from her reflection too."

I put my pillow back and lay down again. I was so angry I didn't sleep until dawn. I woke up at eight and went to the cafeteria for breakfast. Anne was sitting at a table alone. I poured myself some tea and walked up to her.

"There are a few things about last night that I would like to clear up," I said.

"Okay."

I sat down across from her. "I know you have felt invaded by me," I said.

"You're right, I have."

"But my intentions in coming here were pure. I really did feel led to come here, not just to have closure with you, but for a higher purpose, and I was achieving it. If you could just have held me steady, I would have gotten it."

"Gotten what?"

My jaws started to clench. "I would have gotten it. I would have understood the reflection. But instead, you took something I said, created a threatening situation for yourself and pushed me away. Anne, you're looking for a way out of our conversations before I even have a chance to enter them. You…"

"Stop." She put up her hand. "I would appreciate it if you kept this to your own experience. You don't need to take care of me or try to get involved in my issues."

"Fair."

"Fair? What does fair mean?" she asked.

"It means I see where I have done that and you're right, I need to keep this to my own experience of you and not think about what's happening inside of your head."

"Good, that makes me feel a lot better. And you might ask yourself why you feel the need to do that. I need to get some toast, you want some?"

"No, thanks."

She walked over to the toaster. The question was valid. I needed to address why I tried to connect our experiences. She came back and sat down.

"I don't have an answer," I said, "but I'll work on it today."
She nodded.

I continued, "I've been thinking about something you said last night, and I would like to leave you with something to think about."

"Okay."

"I know you'd like to get on with your issues with your boyfriend, but you might find you're looking a gift horse in the mouth. If you would address the issues you have with our relationship, you might find it will bring profound clarity to your other relationship."

She looked as though she'd been hit by the obvious.

I stood up and walked away. "See you later," I said.

She turned toward me and slowly waved me a kiss, and for an instant her eyes went lucid, lit up like reflections of the northern star with a love so powerful, an intelligence so far surpassing what was human that it was clear that God had just appeared through her, incarnated for a brief instant to say: *Congratulations, you made it.*

I walked out bewildered, in awe of the divinity I had just seen, befuddled by days of being ping-ponged between two extremes. I ran into my roommate crossing the bridge, and the moment our eyes met, I burst into tears. The ball had landed on the side of rejection. I felt so unwanted by her that all I could do was sob.

"That's right," she said as she held me tight. "Just let it go, Dawn. Just let it go."

I don't know how long I cried. At one point I tried to pull away, but she sensed I wasn't finished and pulled me closer. At least three more waves of tears rose up from my chest as she firmly rubbed my back, pushing the energy up my spine. When I finished, she held my shoulders and looked into my eyes.

"Life ain't for sissies," she said.

I started to laugh. "You got that right."

I went back to the Big House and found one of the workshop leaders, Gina, sunning herself on the patio. She offered me a seat and I pulled up a chair to face the ocean.

"How's your reunion with your therapist going?"

"Not so good."

"What's going on?"

"I'm not really sure...but there is a part of me that wants to take care of her. She might be sensing that as a trap. And maybe it is."

"Why do you feel the need to take care of her?"

"I guess I'd feel more secure if she needed me, if somehow our experiences were enmeshed."

She nodded. "You know, when children get their boundaries blown open like you had as a child, it's hard to know where you end and somebody else begins. We enmesh with people to comfort a fear."

"What's the fear?"

She smiled. "I don't know. What is it?"

I closed my eyes and pulled it up from the dull pain lingering in my stomach. "I don't want to be abandoned." Tears began to roll down my checks. "Not again."

She put her arm around me. "Then don't leave yourself."

We had the afternoon off, and Paul, Catherine and I went for a hike. We followed the creek into the forest on a red-powdered trail that had worn from the clay. On the edge was a deep green moss that ran through beds of ferns and up the trunks of redwoods. We crossed over a log and walked up the other side where the creek began to pool in large ponds up the path. Paul pointed out the wildlife, doing his best to keep me in the present. Catherine rubbed my shoulders occasionally but let me walk in silence.

I don't buy that. We all hear many voices. It was your decision to act on it.

Anne's words ran through my head a hundred times. She didn't believe me. The woman who showed me faith and love had lost her faith in me. I choked off my tears half a dozen times, kept my eyes on the path and tried to keep moving.

"Look at that tree slug," Paul said. He grabbed a stick and tried to pry the bright yellow creature off the redwood.

Not long ago, I would have helped him, now I pleaded with him to let it be. So sure in my heart that everything has its place and ours was to show reverence, not disruption. He smiled at me and left it alone. We hiked for a couple of hours, then walked back down for dinner. I ate fast and left. I didn't want to see Anne until it was time to say good-bye.

The Thursday night workshop was held in the hot tubs. On the way to the session, I passed by the message board and opened the one with my name on it.

Love is the power through which all things are United.

Love,
Laura

Catherine walked up, and we went down to the hot springs. The group was assembling for what Ted and Gina called an Esalen Indian cleansing ceremony. When we entered the room, we paired up around two massage tables. The tables were piled with coarsely ground salt that our partners were to rub on our skin to cleanse our body of any outer impurities. We then showered and lined up around a large, Roman-style tub where a sacred aromatic oil was dropped into the water for cleansing and a dozen candles were lit around the rim. Ted gestured for silence as we all climbed into the tub. Following his lead, each of us came to the center and submerged for what was considered a cleansing of the past and a re-birthing into the new.

When the silence was broken, we sang, chanted, and dipped in and out of the scared tub. At midnight, when there didn't seem to be an ounce of impurity left in my body, Paul walked me back to the Big House, and I poured myself into bed.

In the morning, I was awakened by a warm sensation in my chest. I rolled over, and just before I opened my eyes, I saw a flash of soft, white light that looked as though it had pushed through a vertical opening in my heart.

I am faith and love.

I opened my eyes as my heart continued to warm and the Light filled my body. I am faith and love. I had taken the path and stayed devoted to my heart. Me. I did it. I was the voice of faith in my head, the loving spirit that had showed me compassion, the guidance that had always been with me. And in that moment, I realized I was not separate from God, but part of God. A branch on Her tree, a ray from His sun. Connected, loved, and accepted for everything I was, everything God had created me to be.

I got out of bed and went into the shower. I rested my head against the wall while the hot water ran down my back. My faith had taken me to Esalen. My love enabled me to survive my childhood. I was the woman I had been looking for. I burst into tears overwhelmed by a sense of gratitude. *Thank you, God. Thank you, thank you, thank you.*

I got out of the shower, wiped the steam off the mirror and looked into my eyes. And I was there. I was me, and I knew who that was.

I dressed and walked down to the living room, grabbed a pen and paper and wrote a note to Anne. I missed her at breakfast, but we were saying goodbye at lunch, so I put the note in my pocket and went in for our final group.

We sat in our sacred circle, happy to be going home, but sad to be leaving each other. There was a pile of small crystals in the center of the room. Ted asked each of us to take a stone and share with the group what we were taking from Esalen.

I went first. I picked up a stone and turned to the group. "I'm taking trust. And I trust that I'm always where I'm supposed to be, with the people I'm supposed to be with. Thank you all very much for helping me through this week."

Paul came to the center of the circle, "I'm taking a new appreciation for life," he said as he turned and nodded to me. "And I fell in love."

I felt a warm flush come up from my chest and a smile swing around my face. His words brought a part of my heart back into light. It was okay to fall in love. To feel your heart come alive with the thought of another person--even if that person was a friend, a therapist, or just somebody you had only known for a week that you knew you would never see again. I put my hands together and bowed to him.

"Thank you, Paul. Thank you."

We took pictures and exchanged addresses, then I said my goodbyes to the group and walked through the gardens to the cafeteria. Passing the message board, I saw a picture of me. I spun on my heels and walked up to a poster on the board as large as the board itself. I stepped closer. It was a collage of my family with a note from Jeff asking Esalen to post it on the board. I pulled it down. There was a picture of Jen and me on the day she was born. *Life's pain can turn into Life's pleasures...* was written underneath in Jeff's handwriting. Next to it was a picture of Maxx running in the water. *Never quit chasing your dreams,* was written below. In the corner was a picture of Matthew asleep in the bottom of an empty swimming pool. *Peace is where you find it...*

I scanned the collage for a picture of Jeff and found him in a photo with the kids. *We are your family* was written underneath. I looked at his image, and my heart came alive at the sight of him. Tears of joy poured down my cheeks. All I wanted to do was to go home to his arms.

There were twenty pictures, all with captions, and each one made me miss my family more. I took the poster into the cafeteria and sat down on a bench. There was a picture of the kids all sitting on a curb. They looked so big. Katie was almost as tall as Matthew, and I couldn't remember the day she grew up, the first time I heard her talk, or saw her walk or crawl across the floor.

Anne walked up, looking to the buffet line and then back at me. I showed her the collage and then went to get a glass of water. When I returned, she was smiling, more present.

"Jeff sent this to you?" she asked.

"Yes, he and the kids must have made it after I left."

We talked about a few of the pictures. I was proud to show them off.

"Fridays are really busy here," she said. "I only have about fifteen minutes."

"That's all right, it won't take that long."

I picked up my poster, and we walked down to the rocks.

"You look happy," she said.

"I am. You weren't the only person I was supposed to meet here."

"I'm glad to hear that," she said. "Do you want to share?"

I looked at her, and a few feet in front of me I suddenly felt the edge of my own boundary. I knew where I ended and she began. I was whole within myself. There was no need to share.

"No," I said. And it felt so good I said it again. "No."

271

She nodded and smiled.

"Well, goodbye," I said.

"That's it! You're ready?"

"Yes, I finally figured it out. I got it this morning."

"It? You keep saying that. What is <u>it</u>?"

I reached in my pocket and handed her the note I wrote.

I got it. I am faith and love.

Thank you,
Dawn.

She read it and shivered. "This gives me goose bumps," she said.

"It gave me goose bumps, too. But this morning, I woke up into it. A flash of light came through my heart and I got it--I realized completely, throughout my whole body that what I saw in you was really in me. This was about me, about my journey, about trusting my path and myself. It was my faith that brought me here and my faith that I would see you again. I am what I saw in you, Anne. And I'll never lose that again."

"I don't really know what to say."

"It's just like the *Wizard of Oz*," I said. "You travel to Oz to find out that what you were looking for, you actually had all along. All you had to do was use it."

"And first you have to go to the witch's castle and deal with the flying monkeys," she said.

"Yeah, and the power to go home was with you all along."

We stood up from the rocks and she handed me the note. "Do you want this back?"

"No. It's for you to keep. I'm at peace with our relationship."

"You are?" she asked looking bewildered.

"Yes, I am." I didn't know why, but I was. I reached over and hugged her.

"Thanks for being my mom," I said.

"You were a good daughter," she replied. "And you make one hell of a woman."

We pulled apart. "You were a good love object to see that in."

She smiled. "I'm glad to hear you say that, because I have something for you, and I wasn't sure how you would receive it. It's a poem that was given to me in a workshop here. I've kept a copy for me, and I made a copy for you. I know it's something I need to keep in mind." She pulled a piece of paper out of her backpack. I opened it up and read it in front of her.

LOVE AFTER LOVE

The time will come
when, with elation,
you will greet yourself arriving

at your own door, in your own mirror,
and each will smile at the other's welcome
and say, sit here. Eat.

You will love again the stranger who was your self.
Give wine. Give bread. Give back your heart
to itself, to the stranger who has loved you

all your life, whom you have ignored
for another, who knows you by heart.
Take down the love letters from the bookshelf,

the photographs, the desperate notes,
peel your own image from the mirror.

Sit. Feast on your life.

--From, Collected Poems by Derek Walcott--

I reach over and hugged her goodbye. "I got it," I said, "I got it."

She put on her backpack and placed her fist over her heart. "You're always here."

I gestured the same. "Always."

"Goodbye, friend."

"Goodbye, Anne." I picked up my poster, jumped in the van and headed home.

A few miles down the coast, I stopped in a small shop and picked up gifts for Jeff and the kids. When, I got back on the road, I realized that I had done what I was sent to Esalen to do. I had received the Light and given it to Anne. All she had to do was accept it. Open the note I gave her and say to herself--*I got it. I am faith and love. Thank you, Dawn.*

When she owned it for herself, she would thank me. And the rejection I had felt from her throughout the week melted into a blissful satisfaction. God comes to us through people. And that pertained to me, too. An hour down the coast my chest warmed, and I heard Anne's voice push through my heart. I got it, she said. I got it.

I rolled into the driveway in the late afternoon. I could hear the kids screaming as soon as I got out of the van. The front door flew open, and they came running out and into my arms. Matthew was the last to barrel into my chest with a force so strong I tipped over onto the lawn. We hugged and rolled onto the grass until Jeff came out and pulled me by my hand into his embrace. I wrapped my arms around his neck and pushed into his body feeling more alive with him than I ever had. He lifted me off the ground and carried me into the house. Jeff put me down and the kids jumped in and out of my arms, running back and forth from their rooms to show me their new treasures from the beach. When they finally settled down, we had dinner, and a few hours later, they were all nestled in their beds. I tucked Jen in last.

"Did you find your friend on your trip?" she asked.

"I did. But guess what else I found?"

"What?" she said as her eyes brightened.

"I found a new love box, and I think it is going to hold a lot more love for everybody."

She started to giggle and curled up on her side. "That's the best thing to find."

"It sure is," I said. "It sure is. Now, sleep tight my little angel."

I went into our room and rubbed Jeff's shoulders in bed while he asked me about my trip. I told him the highlights and how beautiful the grounds were.

"Do you ever think you will see her again?" he asked.

"I doubt it. And honestly, I have no desire to. I was looking for me, not her."

"I could have told you that."

"I think you probably did."

He turned over and pulled me onto his chest.

"And I've been thinking about something else," I said.

"What's that."

"When you're ready. How about it if I become your new girlfriend and we go to the animal shelter and adopt another dog."

"Can we start right now?" he asked as he kissed my neck.

"There is nothing I would love more," I said as I reached up and turned off the light.

CHAPTER FIFTEEN

The wedding day was hectic, as most wedding days tend to be. Matthew was seating guests in the back yard. Jeff was trying to remember how to tie his tie and Katie and Jen were dressing in my bedroom running in and out for various necessities.

Mom, where are your keys," Matthew asked. "I need to move your car so they can drop off Grandma."

"They are in my purse on the counter."

"Does this look straight?" Jeff asked as he walked up behind Matthew.

"It's perfect," I said as I straightened his tie.

"Mom, I need you for a minute," Jen yelled from the bedroom.

"I'll be right there."

Matthew ran back into the kitchen, "Where do you want me to seat Grandma?"

"Put her next to my sister a few rows behind us."

"What if she wants to sit in front?"

"Tell her she can't."

Laura walked in as Matthew walked out looking as if she had barely aged. Still complaining about the baby weight she's been trying to lose for the past twenty years. She put down a gift and hugged me.

"Are you ready for this, mother of the bride?"

I beamed as she spoke. "I'm loving every minute of it."

"Mom, the florist is leaving. They said they need a check."

"It's in the white envelope on the refrigerator."

"Can you help me with this?" Jeff asked as he handed me a white rose boutonniere to pin onto his lapel. I fastened the rose while he whispered in my ear. "Since we are going as each other's date any chance we can... you know..."

I smiled and looked into his light blue eyes. "Sweetie, we're not married anymore."

"That's why it might be more fun," he said as he grinned at me.

"Mooooom!"

"Coming Jen."

I straightened Jeff's lapel, smiled into his eyes, and walked into my bedroom. Jen was standing in front of a full-length mirror. Her long white dress fit snug against her slim body slightly flaring down from her waist. Her face was glowing, framed in long blonde curls and a small line of pearls that dangled from her ears. She was radiant.

"How do I look?"

"Like the most beautiful bride I've ever seen."

"Thanks, Mom. Is Mark here?"

"I saw him about twenty minutes ago. He is a glowing groom."

Laura popped in the room. "It's show time ladies."

"Okay, are you ready?" I asked Jen.

"I'm ready."

We walked back into the living room and Matthew stood up. He was taller than Jeff and even more handsome in his fresh crew cut hair and dark blue suit.

"Sis, you are gorgeous darling. Just gorgeous," he said as he walked up and put his arm around me.

"Isabella!" The kids all screamed in unison as she walked in the door in a light blue flowing dress and her boyfriend by her side.

"Ahhh... Jen... muy bonita." she said with tears in her eyes. Jeff and I went over to hug Isabella when Laura walked back into the room.

"Come on family. It's hot out there in the sun. We need to get started."

"Come on Isabella," Jeff said. "You are sitting next to us."

Katie and Jen picked up their flowers from the counter and hurried out to the front door to meet Jeff at the backyard gate.

"Are you ready, Mom?" Matthew asked.

I paused and took a deep breath. "Just a minute."

I walked back into my bedroom and pulled my orange silk shawl off the edge of the bed and wrapped it around my shoulders. I turned and caught a glimpse of myself in the mirror. And I smiled. Realizing for a moment just how far life had taken me, and how thankful I was for the journey.

"Mom, we need to go," said Matthew.

"I'm ready, Sweetie. I'm ready."

The sun was rapidly descending into the ocean and beads of sweat from the warm summer day shined off the forehead of the classical guitarist. I wrapped my arm around Matthew as he escorted me down the aisle, lined on both sides with friends and relatives. We passed my mother wearing a silk peach dress seated several rows from the front with my sister. My father was at home and not invited to the wedding as he struggled through his final years battling prostate cancer. She smiled at me, and I smiled back. On rare occasions I still saw my mother. When we did speak, we were genuinely kind. I realized long ago that sometimes the best we can do is accept the limitations of others.

Matthew sat me next to an empty chair then took his place at the altar. Katie walked down the aisle next, on the arm of the groom's brother. She looked at me and smiled, then focused her eyes on her boyfriend who was sitting behind me.

The guitarist stopped to alert the crowd, then straightened his back and began a wedding song. Jen emerged from the side yard, escorted by Jeff. She was radiant, and Jeff, the older version of the man I once married, his face ruddy from the sun, his hair still thick and barely greying. He walked Jen to Mark, her groom, and then sat down next to me and reached for my hand. We wove our fingers together as I slid closer to his side.

The words began and the ceremony went by quickly.

"And do you Mark, take Jennifer, to be your wife..." said the women who officiated the wedding.

Mark's hand was shaking as he slid the diamond band onto Jen's finger. Jen then placed a gold band on Mark's.

"Then by the power vested in me by the state of California, I now pronounce you married."

The dancing started shortly after dinner and lasted for hours. I think I only missed one song when I stopped to say goodbye to my mother. I walked her out to her car slowing my pace to meet hers. When I opened the door, she ran her hand down my shawl. "You look so beautiful in this," she said. "Where did you get it?"

"Oh, I've had it a long time," I said as I kissed her on the cheek. "I love you, Mom."

"I love you too, Dawn."

The bride and groom left shortly after midnight and Katie came upstairs to help me clean up the kitchen.

"I finished reading the book you wrote," she said as she put a few coffee mugs in the sink and heated up some tea. "And, I've been wondering about a few things."

"What's that?"

"After you and Dad sold the business, what did you do when the money ran out?"

"I went back to work. A woman I gave the book I wrote invited me to lunch one day. She said she had two executive leaders who were going through some changes, and she thought that I could help them."

"That's how you became an executive coach?"

"Yes. I was able to combine what I learned in therapy with what I knew about business and it became the perfect fit for me."

"That's pretty cool."

"I love what I do. It never feels like work."

She handed me a cup of tea and we sat down at the kitchen table.

"What about Dad. How long after this happened until you got divorced?"

"About 8 years. We went to couple's therapy and tried a few things but ultimately our lives were taking such different paths that it was becoming too painful to stay together." I took a deep breath. "Sometimes the most loving thing we can do for one another is to let each other go."

"He still loves you, Mom."

"And I still love him," I said as I looked through the window to see Jeff, Matthew, and Katie's boyfriend still talking together at the bar.

"Jeff never stopped being my best friend from high school. But he is much happier now living in a fishing village in Mexico. He is where he belongs. And, I have found that it's more natural for me to be with a woman, to write books, support you kids, and to coach people through change. So, I'm where I belong too."

"It doesn't seem like you've dated anyone in a while. Don't you want to be with somebody again?"

"I do, and I'm sure I will someday. But first, I think I need to do something with these messages. I can see the transition starting to happen in the world and people need to understand how important it is to take responsibility for their own healing. We can avoid so much suffering if we embrace who we really are and learn to love more deeply."

"I've been thinking about that," she said, "and I realized something about me."

"What's that?"

"I must be love too." I felt myself beam. "That's right, you are. We all are. We just have to remember and make choices from that center."

"Do you still feel that wholeness you felt when you were at Esalen?"

"I feel forever changed from that week at Esalen. Once you have seen the face of God, the truth is undeniable. It's no longer a belief. It's a knowing. But what is also true, is something the Buddhists say."

"What's that?"

"After the ecstasy, the laundry."

She chuckled. "No, not more work."

"It's true. You come down from those peak experiences into everyday life. You still need to make money to pay for food and housing and to care for your family. And it's not long before everyday thoughts and concerns enshroud you again."

"But weren't you healed?"

"Parts of me were healed, and it certainly deepened my capacity for love and compassion. But healing is not a linear process, and the only cure for child abuse is to stop it from happening. Even embracing the Light does not remove the trauma from the body. I have revisited those scars several times since."

"You've had more abuse memories?"

"Yes, they still get triggered from time to time along with feelings of isolation and worthlessness. It takes a great deal of discipline to remember that we are faith and love when the world is full of such anger and fear. It's going to take the majority of us, bringing our true, and our most loving self into the world before that will change."

"How do we become part of that majority?"

"Commit yourself to it. Our spirit is always trying to heal us, deepen our capacity to love, and guide us to where we can best serve our humanity. We just have to listen and follow our own path. Be willing to do the work to change ourselves."

"And that's how we change the world?"

"The world is already changing. But that is how we will create a gentle transition and avoid an apocalyptic ending. Stop the judgements. Listen to your internal messages. Learn to love yourself, and others, now."

ABOUT THE AUTHOR

Dawn Kohler is a published author and sought-after leadership coach. Her books include an award winning first novel entitled, *The Invitation, A Weekend with Emma,* and *The Messages*, a memoir based on her personal journey and how it relates to the events unfolding in today's world.

For more information about the author please visit her website at *dawnkohler.com*